Blowing My Own Trumpet

Blowing My Own Trumpet

MEMOIRS OF A YORKSHIRE BANDSMAN

COLIN CASSON

TEMPUS

I went through life saying
"I know".
At the end of it, now
I know that I don't know

Jean Gabin, French Actor

First published 2008

Tempus Publishing
Cirencester Road, Chalford,
Stroud, Gloucestershire, GL6 8PE
www.tempus-publishing.com

Tempus Publishing is an imprint of The History Press Ltd

© Colin Casson, 2008

The right of Colin Casson to be identified as the Author
of this work has been asserted in accordance with the
Copyrights, Designs and Patents Act 1988.

British Library Cataloguing in Publication Data.
A catalogue record for this book is available from the British Library.

ISBN 978 0 7524 4719 3

Typesetting and origination by The History Press Ltd
Printed in Great Britain

Contents

Acknowledgements

To my wife Suzie for her tolerance, patience and ever-present encouragement.

Also to Diana, for her persistent, patient persuasion that I should put my stories into writing and for the many hours spent pouring over a computer; and also with grateful thanks to my friend Ian for his assistance and the numerous bottles of red!

With grateful thanks to my brother-in-law Paul Spencer, for the work and time spent turning my memories into book form.

Also thanks must go to: Paul and Jean Greenwood; Peter and Sylvia Kingswood; Susan Caton, Bradford Libraries and Reuben Davison, who never lost confidence is my book being published.

Foreword

Haworth-born like my childhood friend and author of this book, I discovered it when I came over from France where I live now and have taken on French nationality. I taught English in the University & National Polytechnic Institute for 42 years. To my surprise I discovered that Colin had written his memories and, having read the "maquette" I loved the tone, the spontaneity of the style and the interesting accounts of his lifetime travels and passion – THE TRUMPET. As a professor of the Toulouse University I so appreciate this recital of experiences told by as simply and sincerely as anyone could wish. In French we would say 'ÉPATANT'. It is all the more to my taste as I am also in the book at the beginning on a 'Primary School play' at Haworth Infants Section at the age of five disguised as a 'grandma' telling stories to a child at bedtime! I'm very flattered to be able to participate in my own humble way BRAVO COLIN !!!

Sheila A. Can-Todd

Professor of English
ENSEEIHT
University of Toulouse

Introduction

For many years numerous people have encouraged – even insisted – that I write my musical memories. I have always been reluctant and so far declined to do so for several reasons: firstly, I was never a famous personality, and secondly, I considered my life no more interesting than most.

It was after the death of my close colleague and mentor, William Arthur Lang, that his widow Anne made me promise to sit down and write. This I have done.

However, in doing so I have tried to avoid the historical aspects of whichever organisation I have been involved in, concentrating on events from a more personal viewpoint – some happy, some funny, some sad, even tragic moments in my career.

What is between the pages is true. I hope you enjoy reading, whether you be family or friend from the past, present or future. And of course, it's to all musicians!

Colin Casson

one

The early years

As I peered through the blackout windows from my hospital bed in the Eye and Ear Hospital, Bradford, I could see the flashes and hear the muffled explosions of an air raid in the distance.

The year is 1941; I am seven years of age and about to have an operation to remove my tonsils. The whole ward is anticipating that we shall be evacuated to a safer environment, but to our relief the sirens sound the all clear and everything is back to normality.

This moment is one of my earliest recollections, with whips and tops and their beautiful coloured chalky designs, conkers, marbles and all the wonderful games and pastimes long lost to the children of today. Then, the long hazy days of summer, roaming the Yorkshire moors around my home – all a part of my early happy childhood.

I remember how we would go to school with our Mickey Mouse gas masks slung casually over our shoulders, totally oblivious to the fact that they could save our lives. Our footwear was a pair of clogs, if we were lucky! We would see the sparks flying from the 'iron segs' on the causeway. What fun!

On normal routine practices for the expected air raids we kids would sit huddled together in the cold dark atmosphere of the air-raid shelters, shivering with cold and wearing our gas masks. Soon we would hear the voice of Miss Bowker: 'Now children… your four times table…' and we would all begin to chatter away, 'one four is four, two fours are eight…' until the gas masks would steam up and we sat there like creatures from outer space. Then home for the tea – spam fritters, dried eggs, cabbage and sago pudding, not forgetting my favourite: treacle teacakes.

One of my best school friends was Jim Pope, who lived in the police house at the top of Ebor Lane, his father being the local bobby. It was astonishing how our paths would cross during our lifetime…

I was lucky and fortunate to have a good home, albeit only a small cottage under the shadow of the Ebor Textile Mill chimney. Life was always a financial struggle for my parents, but I had love and care, a clean home, a full stomach and an abundance of aunts and uncles.

At the outbreak of the Second World War my father was recalled to the Colours, where he had previously served with the Coldstream Guards in the late 1920s. He was discharged in 1941 because of his age and the fact that he was a skilled machine tool fitter, of which there was a shortage at that particular time.

In the early years of the war it was not uncommon for the local yobs (as they are now called), to be somewhat of a nuisance, with an added touch of verbal abuse, usually directed towards the local women whose husbands were away – some, sadly, never to return.

Haworth Primary School Christmas concert, 1940.

It became apparent that it was our turn to be the victims of their abuse. Usually about nine o'clock a large brick would be hurled at our door. It was dark and during the so-called blackout, when it was compulsory for no lights to be shown whatsoever. My mother and I would sit behind the door nervously anticipating the arrival of the dreaded object.

My father was informed of this on his next leave, and sat behind the door in his khaki trousers, braces hanging to his waist along with his grey Army socks, awaiting the visit of the yobs. To their horror, after releasing their missile a large improperly dressed guardsman appeared in full flight. After a short skirmish a 'prisoner' was brought back, rather bruised and shaken, for interrogation. He was subsequently handed over to the local constabulary, and we settled down again to peace and tranquillity.

Living in a cottage nearby was my little friend Sid Bailey who, like myself, had just started school. 'My dad's going to be a soldier,' said Sid. 'We have to run over to the railway bridge and wave to him on the train'. As the train approached from Haworth Station, Sid's father, Norman, leaned out of the window. 'Look after yourself and behave,' he shouted, disappearing through the steam into the distant Mytholmes Tunnel. Four months later the dreaded telegram arrived containing two black circles: 'It is with deep regret that we have to inform you…'

By today's standards it is hard to imagine the hardships that some people suffered through no fault of their own. Yet with resilience, determination and the will to live they had to keep going. As Sid took his younger sister Norma to school, his mother Alice had already been working in the mill for two hours.

In 1945 the headmaster Mr Roebuck came in to inform us that the war was now over, followed by the most insensitive remark, 'all your fathers will be coming home'. There were tears in Sid's eyes. Unfortunately Sid is no longer with us. After a long career in the RAF followed by a successful engineering business, he was a victim of cancer and died in 2004.

The days seemed to pass endlessly, with balmy evenings and 'old-time dancing' in the local park to the music of the popular Haworth Prize – needless to say – Brass Band.

2653718 Guardsman Casson, the scourge of the local yobs.

Did they really celebrate their win at a famous brass band contest at Belle Vue, Manchester, by playing their instruments as they marched up the main cobbled streets of Haworth in their stockinged feet so as not to waken the sleeping residents?

On another occasion, after an unsuccessful visit to Belle Vue, the band decided to commiserate their disappointment with a visit to a local hostelry. Due to the 'call of nature' on top of the windswept Pennines, the bandsmen stood at the side of the bus. On their return a bass player's wife, who was sitting next to the window proudly wearing her 'pork pie' hat, was heard to say, 'Eh, I were right proud when ours came out!'

Every year there were local Gala Days and I would watch and listen to the band playing as they marched through the village. I was already singing in the school choir and enjoying music, but to see and hear the band inspired me to take up a musical instrument – a brass instrument – and I joined the Haworth band in the beginners' class. The band presented me with an ancient brown portmanteau case and inside was a battered old cornet, positively smelling of verdigris. This was my first instrument and I was very proud to own it.

Haworth church hall, Victory in Europe celebrations, 20 September 1945.

Haworth Band at Oakworth gala.

Me, in my Haworth Band uniform, with my mother.

In those days musical education was extremely basic; a good teacher was a rarity. Most musical advice was built on ignorance and old wives' tales handed down over the years. After a few months of self-teaching, I was given a position on the back row of the Haworth Band. I was allowed to play at a concert held in the Brontë Cinema, where I patiently and excitedly awaited the arrival of the guest soloist – none other than William Arthur Lang, champion cornet player of Great Britain and the then principal cornet of the world-famous Black Dyke Mills Band.

My father, who attended the concert, approached Willie Lang to ask for his advice about a teacher for me. Willie said, 'there's nobody better round here than Tommy Chapman. I played with Tommy in Bradford City Band before the war...' and so started my serious musical education – but not without experiencing some musical politics and petty intrigues, of which I became aware as my career progressed!

There was no doubting the dignity and honesty of the committee members of the Haworth Band. However, it went without saying that any son of a member would get automatic acceptance, on full pay. Sadly this did not apply to me, and after a number of years still on half pay, I decided it was time to move on. After receiving an invitation to join Bradford City Band, I said goodbye to the Haworth Band.

Left: Tommy Chapman.

Below: Tommy Chapman blowing his own trumpet.

Keighley Corporation Parks Committee

BAND Concert | LUND PARK
SUNDAY, JUNE 19th
1949. At 3 & 7-30

Haworth Public Prize Band
Conductor — A. ROGERSON.

AFTERNOON

MARCH	"The Wanderer"	G. Allen
OVERTURE	"Latona."	L. Ham
SELECTION	"Once Upon a Time"	Hume
CORNET DUET	"Besses O'th Barn	D. Carrie
	(T. Chapman and C. Casson).	
FANTASIE	"Hiawatha."	Laurent
VALSE	"Gold and Silver."	F. Lehar
INTERMEZZO	"The Wedding of the Rose."	Jessel
SELECTION	"Cosi-Fan-Tutte."	Mozart
	God Save the King.	

EVENING

MARCH	"Eagle-Ray."	O. Hume
OVERTURE	"Lustspiel."	Kela Bela
SELECTION	"In the Days of Old."	Le Duc
CORNET SOLO	"Babylon."	Adams
—	"Divertimento."	Ball
EUPHONIUM SOLO	"La Belle Americaine."	Hartman
	(G. Beardsley)	
SELECTION	"The Martyrs."	Donizetti
SELECTION	"Crispino."	W. Rimmer
	God Save the King.	

Walter Parker (Keighley) Ltd. Wellington Street, Keighley.

A concert programme for Haworth Band.

two

Moving onwards –
Bradford City Band

One Sunday morning, walking through the room of the Bradford Band Club, I saw in the distance the formidable figure of Fred Berry, famed as conductor of Brighouse and Rastrick Brass Band. At fourteen years of age, Fred appeared to me as a giant of a man, but when I got to know him, he was always softly spoken and he guided me through my short stay as principal cornet at Bradford City, encouraging, advising and educating in the most charming way.

It was apparent that something had to change in my life: school work, homework, school choir and the cornet practice – not to mention the many concerts. My schoolwork suffered and I was taken to account by the dreaded Miss Holdsworth, the music teacher and conductor of the school choir: 'A cornet! A cornet! What's that? You stupid boy! Where's that going to get you?' Many years later I was to find out...

It was at this time that the family moved into a new home in Haworth; a house opposite the family doctor, Dr McCracken. It was a long time before I became aware of the significance surrounding this wonderful man, who had been a surgeon in the Hood Battalion Royal Naval Division during the First World War. Recommended for the Victoria Cross, he was awarded a bar to his DSO.

McCracken had many citations, such as these:

GAVRELLE :
The chief honour went without doubt to Commander Asquith and Commander Bennett, but their efforts were finely seconded by many other officers and men, amongst whom Lt. Commander Funnell (commanding the 189th Machine Gun) and Company Surgeon McCracken R.N. (both of whom were awarded the DSO).

Surgeon McCracken was working under heavy machine gun fire in Gavrelle throughout through the 23rd with the survivors of his own stretcher bearers and a party of German Rd Cross men he had captured. He removed to a cellar for first aid and thence evacuated more than 120 officers and men who would otherwise, in all human probability, have been killed either during the long bombardment or by falling debris. He was recommended by Commander Asquith for the Victoria Cross.

PASSCHENDAELE:
A noticeable feature of almost forty-eight hours continuous fighting by the Hood Battalion, had been the work of Surgeon McCracken DSO who saved the lives of the many wounded, lying out exposed to

Tel. 50.

24 Bilton Road,
RUGBY.

23 May, 1915.

Dear Dr. McCracken,

Thank you very much for the kind letter you wrote to me about my son Sub-Lieut. Rupert Brooke's last illness. I also thank you for the great care and attention you gave him. I am quite sure that you did all for him that you could - it seems quite evident that he hadn't sufficiently recovered his strength after his first illness to resist the final attack.

I was greatly touched at getting a letter from the Men of my Son's Company. As I don't at all know whether the Writer is still alive I send it under cover to you. Would you kindly see that the surviving members of the "A" Coy. get it.

I remain,

Yours sincerely,

M. B. Brooke.

Above: A copy of a letter from Rupert Brooke's mother.

Right: Dr McCracken.

view on the forward slopes of our position under aimed fire from the Passchendaele ridge. From here the enemy has direct, close-range observation of all that was happening on the scene of the attack of the 26th (and the next attack also). The German Field Guns were indeed firing over open sights at every sign of movement.

Surgeon McCracken had been with Hood since the start of the Gallipoli campaign, and his gallantry was a tradition in the Battalion. For his services on this occasion he was awarded a bar to his DSO.

McCracken was subsequently wounded in the head on March 1918.

Not only was he the doctor who attended the poet Rupert Brooke when Brooke died on the Isle of Skyros on the way to the Dardanelles, but he also saved the life of Tiny Freyberg, later Gen. Sir Bernard Freyberg VC, during fighting on the Somme. Dr McCracken's career plummeted somewhat when he brought me into this world!

I began taking further education in the nearby town of Keighley in the Technical College, where Trevor 'Daddy' Day resided. Day was an ex warrant officer, alias geography and history teacher. 'It's a beautiful day for a geography lesson, form up outside in three's. NOW! By the left!' And off would go the class at 120 paces to the minute. 'Keep your dressing, boy!' he would frequently shout. Little did I know that this would be a vitally important experience for me in the not too distant future...

After leaving the college I went to work in the weaving mill in the village near to my home. I continued my studies with the cornet, playing on many occasions in and around the neighbourhood.

three

I join the world-famous Black Dyke Mills Band

'Solo melody contests' were very popular at this time in the North of England. My rendering of *Softly Awakes My Heart* fortunately went down well with the adjudicator at Marsden, near Huddersfield, and I proudly collected my cup.

It was a lucky chance that a talent scout, Alex Mortimer, the celebrated conductor of the Black Dyke Mills Band was in the audience! He asked me to meet with him for a chat. During the chat, Alex Mortimer explained that he was looking for a young cornet player to join the Black Dyke Mills Band in order to take some pressure off Willie Lang as a soloist during afternoon performances. Without any promises I was offered an audition and if successful a chance to play at a band rehearsal.

Tommy Chapman's teaching came to fore, as I had improved my technique and memorized all my scales. The only snag was that I had only just turned fifteen years of age – rather young to join a heavy, first-class outfit such as the BDMB. However, the audition went well and I sat in the band room along with Alex, awaiting the arrival, one by one, of the members of this world-famous band. Needless to say, I was petrified and terribly nervous, but suddenly put at my ease when I saw most of the players wearing boiler suits and overalls, just having left their shift at the mill – at this time you had to work in the Black Dyke Mill in order to have a place in the band. Then in walked the great man himself, Willie Lang, wearing his trade mark 'owl trilby'.

Sitting as fifth man in the top cornet line I was immediately aware of the beautiful and controlled pianissimo playing – something I had never previously been aware of – making me feel as if I were playing a solo. Then my head almost flew off – 'Dyke' were in full flight, with such a change of dynamics.

Owen Bottomley, ex-principal cornet (and didn't we all know it?) spoke to me only three times during my stay with the band. The first time was at the end of my first rehearsal: 'Ah want a word wi' thee. When tha comes in wrong, meck sure tha comes in reight!'

The previous three years had been a highlight in the history of the band – National Champions 1947, 1948 and 1949. After each contest there would be a massed band concert, conducted by Sir Adrian Boult. On one occasion, the father of Buddy Burns, the then soprano cornet player, and just as small as his son in stature, had been celebrating the success of the band, and had had one too many. In his inebriated state, being so proud of his son's contribution, he knocked on the door of Sir Adrian's dressing room. 'What's tha think of ar Buddy, Sir Adrian?'

'Buddy who?' was the reply.

'Buddy Burns – t'soprano wi't' Dyke.'

'Oh, jolly good,' was Sir Adrian's reply.

'Jolly good? Ee's t'best bloody Soprano in t'world,' retorted Buddy's father.

Black Dyke Mills Band, champions again.

Sir Malcolm Sargent advising Kenny Pinches and myself.

THE SAM DUGDALE TRUST

presents a

MUSICAL EVENING

Organised by the Fairlea Choir

in the

CO-OPERATIVE HALL, Luddendenfoot,

Wednesday, March 4th, 1953

To Commence at 7-30 p.m.

ARTISTES:

BLACK DYKE MILLS BAND QUARTET
WILLIAM A. LANG, - - - **Cornet**
COLIN CASSON - - - **Cornet**
GORDON E. SUTCLIFFE - - - **Horn**
GEOFFREY WHITHAM - **Euphonium**
Conductor: **ALEX MORTIMER**

FREDERICK NOBLE - - - **Baritone**
B.B.C. London and Provincial Concert Artiste.

FAIRLEA CHOIR - Winners Local Festivals

Conductor: **Madame FLORENCE BOOTH**
Accompanist - **Mr. ARNOLD MARSHALL**

ADMISSION FREE

COLLECTION [Silver desired] at the door
Proceeds for Fairlea Choir Funds

J. D. Broadbent. Printer, Ripponden. Tel. 2273

A concert programme with Black Dyke's quartet.

150th anniversary concert with ex-members, Huddersfield Town Hall, 2005.

Another duet, in Harrogate, fifty years later.

four

Life in t' mill

As previously mentioned, if you were to play with the Black Dyke Band you had to work 'in t' mill'! Most of the jobs were of a semi-skilled or labouring nature. Ostensibly because of the long absences during the summer months and time lost for concerts and broadcasts, I was given a job in the warp dressing and twisting department, supposedly as an apprentice. However, most of my apprentice work amounted to sweeping the floor, 'reaching in' (a part of the textile process) and other menial tasks. Sometimes I moved the very heavy warps to and from the waiting lorries.

I travelled each day from my village on an old Brontë bus; the driver was called Joe Birdsall. Joe would collect me from Haworth Station and deliver me to the mill at Queensbury, some five miles away. I had to be at the station at 6.15 a.m. where, together with other workers, we all piled into the bus. The bus windows quickly steamed up with the blue smoke from tobacco and jokes! I had to pay Joe 2s 6d in old currency for the week's transport – it seemed a lot of money to me out of my weekly £2 pay!

We had to 'clock on' in the mill by 7.00 a.m., where Horace Johnson, the departmental manager, would be waiting. He was small in stature, with a pasty complexion (which most had), boots turned up at the toes and trousers at half mast – the uniform of the day.

Horace was the mill 'bookie', illegal in those days. He wore a flat cap which could be removed so rapidly, for scratching purposes, that one could never see the top of his head. Horace lived in mortal fear of Galimore, the managing director, who presided over all three floors above. Horace would place his spies and informers to tell him in advance of any surprise visit. He would sweat profusely at the mere thought of Galimore's questions. There would be up to twelve individuals residing in this dark and uninviting part of the mill, where electricity was sparse to say the least.

Pint pots could be seen on the window ledges waiting for whoever's turn it was to make the tea, usually around 8.45 a.m. One of the occupants, a young lady who came from Durham, never wore any knickers and would frequently lift her skirts for the benefit of those around.

Old Bill, a rather greasy individual, would sit on his buffet chewing black twist and occasionally cutting off the weft from the 'heald' (another textile term), throwing it into a corner, followed by the usual blob of twist. Sitting opposite Old Bill, also on a buffet, knees almost touching and ready to place an 'end' from the warp onto his hook, was this young lady. This was a procedure called 'reaching in'.

Inside the weaving shed of Ebor Mill, Haworth.

On one occasion when I had been standing around with nothing in particular to do I watched this process with interest. Old Bill decided to change hands, which had been manoeuvring repeatedly inside the lady's skirt, causing her to rotate her eyeballs excitedly. Some fifteen minutes later a voice could be heard asking whose turn was it to make the tea. Suddenly Old Bill appeared with three pint pots in each hand, the contents of which were splashing over his fingers. I declined the offer of the morning tea that day!

At lunch time, there was food made available in one of the less salubrious parts of the dark mill interior for those desperate enough to risk it! Sometimes I would walk down for lunch with a young Ukrainian lad whose name was Pitch. He worked in a loading bay not far from my station. The routine was to load a heavy warp into a lift and either to quickly jump in the lift to travel to a different level, or to sprint up the stairs in order to meet the lift and warp which would then be loaded onto a wagon. Sadly, Pitch paid the ultimate price one day when he jumped but did not clear the entrance of the lift and was killed outright – something that has stayed with me all my life.

five

A glimpse into the future

By this time I had saved enough money to acquire a BSA Bantam motorbike which made my life much easier travelling to and from work and especially returning from late-night concerts.

One of the finest exponents of the euphonium was Geoffrey Whitham. He and his parents could be described as 'big people with big hearts'. Harold Whitham, Geoff's father, drove a flour wagon and normally created a cloud of white powder whenever he dashed his flat cap. Harold was a regular and devoted 'Pondasher'. (Where this word originated no one knows, but it means a Black Dyke supporter.)

Sometimes, returning very late from a 'gig', I would stay with the Whitham family, where Mrs Whitham would have a fish supper awaiting for us in the oven. Even after only a few hours sleep we would clock in on time for a full day's work and I could look forward to Horace giving me a bulging wage packet of £2 10s each Friday.

Whenever the band played at shows or galas there would be the inevitable spread of sandwiches and cakes for refreshments. At one particular venue, Reeth Show, in North Yorkshire, the spread was set out in the corner of a small marquee. Sitting alone was one fresh cream horn; this was immediately snatched by Owen Bottomley, the cornet player. 'That bugger's mine,' he said, spitting on to the cake as he spoke. A fellow musician, Arthur Oldfield, who held position of third cornet for thirty years, picked up the wretched cake, saying, 'tha can bloody 'ave it!' and christening it with his own spittle.

One 'gig' was at New Brighton and during a break I took the opportunity of visiting a fairground, where there was a fortune teller, one Gipsy Rose Lee. My main concern in life at that time was whether or not the band would win the forthcoming National Championship, so I consulted with Gypsy Rose Lee. 'I see lots of blue sky and sea...' she said, reading my palm, 'and there will be lots of travel where you will eventually meet a dark-haired young lady'. After a pause, she said, 'Wait a minute! I also can see a very young light-haired person in the distance...'

Having no satisfaction regarding the outcome of the contest, I returned to fulfil my duties with the band. Little did I realise the lasting effect Gypsy Rose Lee's reading would have on my life, even if she could not tell me the result of the championship! As rehearsals progressed in preparation for the forthcoming National Championships, the test piece being on this occasion *Epic Symphony* by Percy Fletcher, it meant many long hours of extensive practice. The piece never seemed to come together. It was difficult – but then they usually were – but on the last day before the contest, it all came together.

Geoffrey Whitham, with a euphonium.

If there were other Yorkshire bands competing in the same contest it was to be expected that there would be spies, such as an unexpected visitor, more often than not from our common foe 'Brighouse and Rastrick'. Their intent would be to learn of another band's interpretation and treatment of the set piece. More musical intrigue!

After an early breakfast at the Royal Hotel, Russell Square, we left for a final rehearsal before taking part in the contest. The band had been barred from competing in the Daily Herald National Brass Band Championships the previous year because of their three successive victories in earlier years. Tension was terrific, especially the last-minute nerves moments before entering this vast arena, which would be full of supporters, enthusiasts and those peculiar individuals all waiting in anticipation for the slightest mistake.

We played and then we had to await the decision of the panel of adjudicators, who were hidden out of sight of all the performances, so as not to be influenced. It was an anxious and electrifying period waiting for the results; it had been a hotly contested championship and all taking part had played well. The results, announced by John Snagge of the BBC, 'in reverse order, Fairey Aviation, Brighouse and Rastrick, Foden's Motor Works... and the winners... BLACK DYKE MILLS BAND'. We had done it again!

And so we returned to the North of England and to Queensbury, the home of the band, arriving at 5.15 p.m. on Monday – just in time for the victory march to the Stags Head public house, together with all the mill workers joining in the celebrations. A short impromptu concert would normally take place, but then, after the excitement of the band's successful journey to London, life would return to the drab existence of the daily routine in the mill.

On the announcement of our success, 1951.

A celebration concert for the mill, on our return from London.

Black Dyke leaving for a southern tour, 1952.

Cornet duet with Willie Lang and the author, St Helier, Jersey, 1953.

> *To whom it may concern.*
>
> I have great pleasure in giving Colin Casson this testimonial.
>
> He has played beside me as assistant Principal cornet for the past two years, and throughout that time I have found him most conscientious and co-operative.
>
> I have no doubts whatsoever; given an opportunity he will make a name for himself as a cornetist.
>
> W. Lang.
> Principal Cornet.
> Black Dyke Mills Band.
> Queensbury.
> Yorkshire.

A testimonial letter given to me by Willie Lang.

The normal summer diary for the band would be the ever-popular seaside resorts such as Eastbourne and Worthing, with visits to Devon, Cornwall and South Wales. One particular year, our conductor Alex Mortimer informed the band that the evening concert would be held in the open air in a rugby field. The opening march, the band's own signature tune 'Queensbury', was to be conducted by the retired musical director of the Grenadier Guards, Lt-Col. Miller, who had recently retired to Helston, where we were to play.

That evening as we were ready to start the colonel approached the rostrum, taking up the baton. 'Are you frightened of me, gentlemen?' A fellow cornet player, Kenny Pinches, normally a quiet and reserved character, replied, 'Are we f★★k! 'Ow abaht thee?'

Kenny was one of four brothers who had played with the band. One of the brothers, Alwyn, was still playing with the band at that time. Jack, another brother, was playing with the BBC Symphony Orchestra and Harold, the youngest brother, was killed in action with the Guards Armoured Division. Their father, Harold Pinches, was a legendary principal cornet player.

After a concert in Barnsley, Mortimer, in one of his usual moods, insisted that the bus went straight to the band room on arrival in Queensbury. Mortimer's ruling was extremely unpopular, as the usual custom of dropping off the band players as near their homes as possible was ignored. This attitude, along with the disciplines upon which Mortimer insisted, had now reached an unacceptable level. The brothers Pinches could take no more and proceeded to manhandle Mortimer, covering him with their greatcoats and instruments. Mortimer was subjected to an ignominious 'Goodnight'! This event culminated in the sad exit from the band of the two brothers and an untimely end to their musical careers. The Mortimer regime resulted in many good players leaving the band. The standard of playing suffered and was not to improve until the late fifties/early sixties, under a new leader.

Although Mortimer ruled with a rod of iron and was at times unreasonable, he was a brilliant band trainer and teacher. I myself owe a debt of gratitude to him for the help he gave me in my early years.

A fellow cornet player with the band, Peter Hey, had recently completed his apprenticeship as a weaving over-looker. He approached me one day with the suggestion that the two of us should join the Army. He had learnt that the Black Watch were advertising for recruits. I declined the offer immediately, as I could not imagine anything worse! Peter went ahead with his plan and I wished him well in his new venture.

Another band engagement was a *Television Spectacular*, starring Gracie Fields and including the comedian Albert Modley, Donald Peers (of Babbling Brook fame) and us. The band stood for most of the time at the back of the stage in the Grand Theatre, Leeds. After singing, Donald Peers announced that he wished to introduce a young up-and-coming singer, and on to the stage walked Frankie Vaughan.

In one of the ashtrays (sorry, boxes) sat the boxer, Randolph Turpin, who had recently beaten Sugar Ray Robinson for the World Middle Weight Championship. During an interval, a couple of us went to ask Randolph Turpin for his autograph. We were confronted by a large pugilistic gentleman and Mr Turpin turned to the 'minder' saying, 'Tell them to f★★k off!' We did! Faster than Turpin could turn around in his seat!

One of my good friends during my time at Black Dyke was Tommy Waterman. Tommy played soprano cornet. He had come up North from Leamington Spa and had been educated at Loughborough College. Because of this education, he was given a job in the mill as a colour matcher! A job far superior to the normal menial jobs handed to band players. Unfortunately Tommy suffered very badly with asthma, which would occasionally result in him missing a concert. Tommy and I had an altercation during a journey to a 'gig' and had to be separated by Bill Lang. This did not go unnoticed and was to be brought to my attention in the not too distant future…

Most of us in the band at that time had nicknames: Tommy's was 'Scatliffe'. Scatliffe was a famous soprano cornet player in the early 1920s. It was also a name synonymous with the approaching end of my time with Black Dyke Mill and the band. In August 1953 we played a week in St Helier, Jersey. Evening concerts were held in the Howard Davies Park, and there was a morning performance in the town centre. As we all assembled for breakfast in the Franks Private Hotel, Willie Lang was in the mood for one of his famous pranks. Scatliffe (Tommy), being the last one down to breakfast, was the subject of the prank on this occasion. Willie spoke in a loud voice for all to hear: '…So we all agree! The soloists are to receive one pound extra, and Colin gets ten bob for playing duets with me.'

'What about me?' asked Scatliffe. 'I'm the soprano and soloist as well.'

'No! Sorry,' said Willie. But the joke backfired as Scatliffe turned up late for both morning and evening shows. Even an eventual explanation that it was merely a joke did not convince Tommy and the foolhardy atmosphere lingered on with us for some time.

On our return to Queensbury I was summoned immediately to the office of Alex Mortimer. He flew into a rage, accusing me of being a troublemaker, exacerbating Tommy's illness with my barrack-room lawyer's attitude. I was told that this, culminating with the 'incidents' in Jersey, would not be tolerated. I tried to explain to Mortimer that the incident to which he was referring was not of my making and that I was totally innocent of the allegations. 'If as you say you are innocent, then who was the instigator?' asked Mortimer. I was not willing to disclose this information and had no other option but to remain under suspicion of guilt. It was not until many years later and when Bill Lang was in his eightieth year that I explained the reason for my leaving the band.

On the day I resigned I took my band uniform and instrument to Mortimer's office. I thanked him for all he had done for me over the years, but sadly Mortimer chose to ignore me – a sad ending to three and a half happy years. I said farewell to my work and band mates. Even Owen Bottomley made some gesture at my leaving.

Back at the mill Old Bill, still spitting his black twist into the pile of weft, nodded at me for my attention to it and suggested that I should pick it up. I politely, but firmly, told him where to put it, and was immediately threatened with dismissal if I did not comply. And so it was goodbye to all that. It was well worth the experience and I would not have missed it.

Having recently undergone the compulsory medical examination and been pronounced fit and A1, I reluctantly accepted my fate, left BDM and the band behind me and prepared myself for a military career. I spent an enjoyable week with my loving parents before catching a train to London and then on to a place in Surrey called Caterham and the shock of my life…

six

Join the Micks and go to Hollywood, they said…

Life in the raw! Caterham guards depot, Surrey. For all the unfortunate candidates that missed the entrance to the lunatic asylum, which was situated next door to the barracks, it would be an experience never to be forgotten.

At 10.00 p.m. on a foggy night in November 1953, I arrived at the intimidating barrack gates. A khaki-clad statue with forage cap and neb over his chin stood with fixed bayonet. Was he real? The thought that crossed my mind was to turn and run as far and as fast as possible away from this place. A scream pierced the air and an apparition appeared through the mist. There was obviously no control of the decibel level here!

'Joining the brigade?'

'Sir?' I replied.

'The f★★★ing guards?'

'Yes sir!'

'Which one?'

'Irish Guards, sir'

The apparition shouted for the orderly, who replied 'sergeant!'

'Take 'im to the receiving room, draw some bedding on the way.' Then, turning to me, 'Follow 'im… double quick time… left, right, left… MOVE!' I took off with my new-found friend, down the leafy drive boarding the infamous parade ground with its foreboding drill sheds. After drawing two sheets and three smelly blankets, we arrived at the barrack room known as the receiving centre, where other new club members were sitting on their respective beds, some smoking, some cursing and some whimpering. 'Make your bed up over there!' I was told by the lance corporal. So here we were, all mixed up and waiting to be segregated into our different regiments. What surprises awaited us!

Sitting on the bed next to me was a young lad from Devon who was going to join the Grenadier Guards. He was National Service recruit as were most of the lads and he did not seem to be too keen on the idea. I told him that I had signed up for three years as I was hoping eventually to be transferred into the Regimental Band.

The lights went out and a cockney Teddy boy from a bed opposite came over and took a blanket from the bed of the young Devon boy. It was very cold and there was no heating in the barrack room – so cold that a frost was glistening on the inside of the windows. The poor quivering lad's request to have his blanket returned met with a point-blank refusal and the Londoner pulled out a stiletto knife. 'Come and get it if you want it,' he said menacingly.

This was a completely new experience for most of us, having left our homes at such young ages. What happened next I shall never forget; a well-made young lad from Huddersfield crossed the room towards the Londoner, managed to deflect the blade of the stiletto knife and followed through with a left hook that knocked the Teddy boy clean over his bed. The blanket was returned and we all slept fitfully. The courage that was shown that night was worth a medal.

My work experience obtained during the years in the textile mill came into good use during the next week in the receiving room – general cleaning, scrubbing floors and carrying heavy loads of coal to the officers' quarters. Shades of my time at the mill!

It was not long before I joined Sgt Fawcett's squad. He sported a handlebar moustache and was a strict, but fair, gentleman and an excellent drill instructor.

The forming of the squad was the responsibility of Full Sgt O'Flynn who, it was reputed, had served in the intelligence department of the Irish Guards. In his Belfast brogue he shouted, 'Get in a line… alphabetical order, and call out your names'. Suddenly the line stopped. 'What's your name?' asked O'Flynn. 'Phillips, sergeant,' came the reply. 'What are you doing in the Ps then? Get in the f***ing Fs!'

Part of the structure of barrack room life was to have a trained soldier (a guardsman) living with the squad to show how things worked – cleaning kit and early necessities of Army life. He always had to be addressed as 'trained soldier' – 'Permission to enter the room, trained soldier.' 'Permission to leave the room, trained soldier.' We had the honour of a trained soldier by the name of Kenealy, whose bed was next to the fire for obvious reasons. A certain odour would permeate the air when he was about – definitely not Yves St Laurent. The smell of old socks, sweat and Blanco made it quite obvious that he had been around for some time.

Rising at 5.00 a.m. each morning, marching in threes with towels tucked under the right arm, we headed for the swimming baths, passing the dreaded 'Jacksy' company sergeant major shaving outside his hut, oblivious to the weather conditions. He could often be seen carrying out his ablutions whilst covered in snowflakes. The glass windows covering the pool were usually open, thus allowing a film of ice to cover the surface of the pool. Some thirty or so naked prospective warriors and one bandsman were waiting to break the ice.

A large pile of wet and frozen denims were piled in a corner waiting to be worn, just for our comfort. Feeling exhilarated, we would march back just in time to scrub the barrack room floor and prepare beds for inspection, awaiting the inevitable reveille at 7.00 a.m.

Then breakfast time when, once again, in threes, each one carrying an enamel mug and eating utensils, we approached the cook houses with a hunger and desire to eat anything provided. Bottles of HP brown sauce stood on long wooden tables that led to the collection department where the chefs, wearing their long, white, crisply laundered hats and resembling something from the *Wizard of Oz*, awaited our arrival. These were the culinary gentlemen who were responsible for feeding us: they stood menacingly behind enormous steaming steel basins. Usually the food landed intact on the plate, but quite often it would ricochet off the side of the steel bowl, followed by a growled 'move on!' Any request for something different would be met by the response 'f**k off!', which we took to mean no!

A brisk run around Coulsdon Common in 'small pack', followed by more drill, looking forward to 'shining parade' in the evening, was the normal daily routine. The only relief to look forward to was the time allowed to sit on your bed in the evenings listening to the friendly banter of one's comrades and the *Forces Network* on the radio.

After six weeks of square bashing we were allowed Christmas leave. On reflection I can't believe that Santa would have been too happy in this place! An inspection just before we took our Christmas leave gave O'Flynn the opportunity of wishing me well, spitting in my face something about not being too happy about the cleanliness of my capstar – 'and a Merry Christmas to you, too,' were my thoughts.

Following a happy Christmas time with my family back in Yorkshire, I had to face the reluctant return to my new family in Caterham. On arrival I changed into my regulation denims, but realized I had forgotten to hand in my leave pass. 'Better go back and hand it in,' was the advice from Trained Soldier Kenealy. To my horror, most of the buttons on my denims were missing and when I entered the guard room, I was confronted by two ugly looking Welsh Guards corporals. They immediately started to prod my person with their canes. This was not an enjoyable experience and I began to feel weak at the knees with a sickly feeling in the pit of my stomach. What was going to happen now? The corporals muttered something in a language unknown to me at the time, and proceeded to open the iron door leading to a cell. I was pushed and kicked into the cell, which was dark, dank and very smelly. Struggling to see in the half light I bumped into what seemed to be a wooden butcher's block. Here I sat for the next three hours in complete darkness, when eventually at around 3.00 a.m. the door opened. Not for my release – they had not finished with me…

I felt a blow from behind, which knocked me to the floor, and then the canes came into further use… 'Like a dog! Like a dog boyo! Woof!' I had no alternative but to satisfy their demands and I was gratefully booted out into the night. My memories are that it was a clear starlit night. I have often thought of what happened to me that night and why.

To have reported this treatment would have been futile and dangerous for me during my stay. This did not happen just to me; the brutality and bullying was a regular well-known occurrence, to which the superior officers turned a blind eye. Part of Army life? Possibly, and it quite likely goes on to this day.

I returned to my cold bed thinking, 'You can take it Casson… remember the old Black Dyke motto, "*Nil desperandum illigitimus carborundum*" – don't give up, don't let the b★★★★★★★s grind you down!'

seven

Life in the Guards

It wasn't long afterwards that I received the orders to be posted to the Regimental Band of the Irish Guards and London duties. I was happy to leave Caterham behind and departed in full marching order. On arrival in London, I was met at Sloane Square by Cpl Bob Horton, principal flute in the Regimental Band. We travelled together to Wellington Barracks, Birdcage Walk, which was to be my home for a while.

Here I was introduced to the famous 'Jiggs' – Capt. C.H. Jaeger, director of music, Band of Her Majesty's Irish Guards. His lovely wife Eileen, a Yorkshire lass, made me tea and 'Jiggs' offered me the position of principal cornet with the Regimental Band – a far cry from my reception at Caterham on a cold November night. Still at the tender age of eighteen, I had arrived in London, with a place in the Irish Guards, and elevated to principal cornet.

The Regimental Band sergeant major was Col. Sgt Frank Clark, senior band sergeant, Major Brigade of Guards. He was a man of 6ft 7in stature in his stocking feet, rising to 9ft in his bearskin – certainly a man to look up to. Like all 'Clarks', he was known by the nickname Nobby. His chosen instrument was the BIG drum. He sported a large blue nose, due to prolific Bass drinking, which contributed to another nickname of 'Brown Boots Clark', following an accident that befell him some years previously while taking part in Trooping the Colour.

Thursday was payday and Nobby took the opportunity of giving out future orders, sometimes announcing odd 'gigs', which filtered through to those individuals who showed interest. One such day, exactly one month after my arrival in London, Nobby announced that there was a gig, stating 'trumpet required! Geraldo Enterprises! Anybody interested?' This met with silence, then a quiet, 'Yes sir'.

'What! You, son?'

'Yes Sir!'

I was given a telephone number to call, but was aware of several titters, smiles and mumblings from the ranks…

I was the proud owner of an old, battered 'Boosey' trumpet, which had come into my possession before I left home. I had just celebrated my eighteenth birthday and I was ready to go. What the hell, I thought; it would probably be in a Town Hall in Chelsea or Fulham, playing in a five- or six-piece gig…

When I made the call the secretary of Geraldo Enterprises informed me that 'Darky Hutchinson' had left their band and they needed a stand-in deputy for the forthcoming Saturday night. I was asked if I could be at Broadcasting House, Piccadilly, at 4 p.m. that day. I said that

A newspaper advert for a forthcoming concert.

I had not done any busking, improvising that is, and her reply was, 'Sorry! Can't what? Don't worry! Is four o'clock okay for you?' Of course I said yes!

There were a number of broadcasting venues in Piccadilly at that time and as I walked from one to the other a band bus pulled up. 'Are you trumpet, mate, Geraldo?' I was asked. 'Yes I am,' I replied, and I was invited to 'hop on then!' I sat next to one of the band's regular singers and asked him where the bus was taking us. 'Peterborough corn exchange,' was the reply, then, 'here's Delaney,' as Eric Delaney got on the bus.

As the bus left London, travelling up the Edgware Road, it dawned on me that it was the wrong time, wrong day and certainly the wrong band. But it was too late! We arrived at the corn exchange in Peterborough and the dance was soon filled. I was stuck on the end of the trumpet section with my immediate partner being Derek Abbott, a great jazz trumpet player. When Derek saw my little battered tin mute he offered to share his!

Jill Day was the female singer and she came on stage followed by the man himself – 'Geraldo'. Then my agony started. Sections would stand as a man and then sit, leaving one standing to take a short flourish. For the first half of the dance programme I found myself standing or sitting, but all at the wrong time and on occasion standing alone, but not a sound coming from my bell end. And all this time Geraldo would be glaring in my direction. I tried not to catch his eye, but I knew what he was thinking – who IS this guy? If only the hole, which I longed for, would open up and swallow me whole.

Myself, recently elevated to corporal.

At the interval I found myself signing autographs along with Eric Delaney and just for a fleeting moment basked in the glory and the happiness I was convinced had eluded me. The second half of the programme was all exhibition – no dancing – with all musical arrangements by Eric Delaney; *The Sky's the Limit* and *The Hawk Talks* were just a couple. By this time Geraldo's infamous smile had disappeared and was replaced by a frown every time he looked in my direction. The agony continued until midnight and during the return trip to London I tried my best to hide under a seat on the bus. When we eventually arrived at Piccadilly I said a sheepish farewell to my band mates of the evening before making a speedy exit to Wellington Barracks. All was quiet and the barracks were in darkness, just a sergeant and sentry on duty. The peace was shattered: 'Where the f★★k have you been?'

'You would never believe it sergeant,' I replied; 'Good Night.' And I went to my bed.

Exactly one week later I received a cheque for £5... not bad for a night's work.

eight

Life in Wellington Barracks

Cleanliness and tidiness were of prime importance in our barrack room, which had been especially allocated to the brigade bandsmen. At that time I became very friendly with the clarinet player, Keith Binns, who was serving in the Coldstream Guards. After a while Keith and I were given a living-out allowance and found a small room at No. 147 Alderney Street, Pimlico.

Keith had a brother called Malcolm who was an accomplished pianist, then serving with the Royal Signals Band. Many years later, when I was living and working with the BBC Welsh Symphony Orchestra, Malcolm and I performed Shostakovich's *Trumpet and Piano Concerto* with Rudolph Schwartz conducting.

Back in our room in Pimlico, we were provided with a small cooker and our culinary expertise became legendary with the popular dish of bean porridge! A combination of breakfast and evening presentation – not to be missed!

In the same house resided Ruth. Ruth's room was as small as ours, but she was privileged to have the room for sole occupancy. Ruth came from Liverpool and was working in a library in Victoria, London. Ruth and Keith became good friends, eventually marrying – a relationship still going strong to this day after fifty years!

I soon was to learn the art of 'street lining' as a regular part of a bandsman's duties. Any visiting monarch, prime minister or head of state would qualify for a state visit and this would involve any of the regiments being selected for street-lining duties.

On one occasion the Irish Guards, known colloquially as 'The Micks', were formed up alongside the Royal Welsh Fusiliers Band, whose 'big drummer' was a rather large gentleman emanating from one of the Caribbean islands. Unlike the Guards, who would wear red aprons, this gentleman had his big drum hooked on to a leopard skin. The RSM of the Guards, being in charge, wandered about with his pace stick (as they were prone to do) checking the last-minute details. On seeing the drummer he approached the gentleman and exercised his usual humour: 'Who told you to come in civvies?' he asked.

Next on the agenda would be spring drills, which usually started in late April, in preparation for the Trooping of the Colour to celebrate the Queen's official birthday in June. Each band would drill independently, culminating in the massed formation nearer the time of the Trooping. On one particular occasion our Regimental Quarter Master Sgt Stewart was in charge of proceedings, when the director of music, 'Jiggs' Jaeger, appeared round the corner. 'Good morning RQMS,' was the greeting. 'Good morning sir,' replied RQMS Stewart, who started to indulge in conversation with the director. The band were already on the move, marching in six ranks and heading straight for a truck which had been delivering desks to the education department. With no further orders the left three ranks marched up the ramp of the truck and immediately started to mark time... the rest of us kept marching until the order of 'HALT!' from a rather shocked and somewhat embarrassed RQMS brought us to a standstill. Exhausted and sweating, thankful that the drill had ended, a voice from the ranks was heard to say 'how sweet a thing is death!'

'Who said that?' exclaimed the frustrated RQMS.

The same voiced replied, 'Actually it was Shelley, sir!'

nine

Trooping the Colour – 1954

This was to the first of many for Queen Elizabeth and the first of seven for yours truly.

The routine of the day was of paramount importance. A good breakfast was essential, followed by a visit to the toilet, which was of equal importance. We were all provided with glucose sweets to help us through the long morning. One piece of advice from the longer-serving members of the regiments was 'watch out for Hell Fire Corner!' When asked for an explanation of Hell Fire Corner the usual response would be, 'You will soon find out!'

A very difficult manoeuvre which takes place during the ceremony of Trooping is called the 'spin wheel', which is performed by the massed bands, pipes and drums, marching thirty abreast and turning on its own base – no mean feat. We made it look simple, but only after hours of rehearsing. There is no written order and it has been handed down over hundreds of years through word of mouth: it can be a nightmare for new, raw recruits, who have been known to get lost in the melee. The only way out is to ask a fellow bandsman 'which way do I go?' The reply would be, 'Turn left at the lights…', but then a helpful hand gently on the shoulder would guide the unfortunate individual in the right direction.

On the conclusion of the event, the Queen, along with her Household Cavalry, mounted on their magnificent horses with gleaming coats and the sun flashing from the burnished breast plates of the Troopers, head down The Mall towards Buckingham Palace. Then it becomes the Foot Guards' turn to follow, when a wet, steaming and odious object can be felt hitting the back of the neck, usually projected by the toecap of an Army boot from the gentleman marching behind. A present from the Household Cavalry – and the meaning of Hell Fire Corner becomes apparent.

Open ranks across The Mall and down to the palace for an hour's musical rendition of regimental music; then the final march off and dismissal, with a mouth like the Dalai Lama's flip-flops and covered in horse s★★t – it wasn't too bad an experience after all.

We were often invited to take part in radio broadcast engagements, and on one of these occasions, which was being recorded at Farringdon Street, London, I was to play the cornet solo 'shylock'. During the rehearsals for the broadcast a voice was heard saying, 'Is that little Colin Casson from Ebor Lane, Haworth?' To my surprise it was Jim Pope, my old school friend, who was a trainee sound mixer working for the BBC. This was the first of the coincidental meetings we had over the years.

On one occasion, at the Order of the Bath Ceremony, Westminster Abbey, six trumpeters – three at each side of large pillars – were way up in the rafters of the abbey. As the director of music was indisposed, Band Sgt Maj. Nobby Clark was in charge of the musical part of the proceedings.

The Queen's first Trooping the Colour, 1954.

He had placed himself in a position where he had sight of the arrival of the Queen and her entourage. Unfortunately, all we trumpeters could see was Nobby's hand, and we missed the all-important cue. The next thing that was heard was Nobby's loud voice screaming, 'For Christ's sake... FANFARE!' and this cry reverberated and echoed all around the upper echelons of the abbey... It wasn't long afterwards that Nobby retired gracefully, after many years of distinguished service in the Brigade of Guards and The BIG drum.

Mrs Druery was the widow of RSM Druery, Coldstream Guards; an elderly and popular landlady with the older members of the band. She ran a small hotel in Eastbourne, primarily for the visiting bands. It had been suggested that I join a party of fellow musicians who had enjoyed Mrs Druery's care and attention on previous occasions. I was lucky: there was a room available. Mrs Druery showed me to my room addressing me as 'Casson' and asking me if I wanted a chamber pot! I asked Mrs Druery if I could have a key to the front door as it was my intention to go dancing on the pier after the concert had finished. Judging from her reaction this would appear to be an unusual request as she very reluctantly produced a key.

It was late and dark when I returned to the house and to my horror the key broke in the lock. There I stood in full dress uniform not knowing what to do when I saw that the dining room window was ajar. I opened the window and climbed in onto a table set and prepared for breakfast. The table collapsed and I rolled off onto a sofa – and on top of a sleeping body, which turned out to be none other than the amenable landlady, Mrs Druery.

Nobby Clarke and his big drum.

Princess Marina and Princess
Alexandra opening the Canadian
National Exhibition.

She awoke with alarm and accused me of being a sexual pervert, surprised that a young and supposedly innocent person had such machinations. I was just as horrified and dismayed when she told me she would report my actions to my commanding officer the following day. I tried in vain to explain that the key had broken in the lock but she refused to accept my story until the following morning when she discovered the offending key well and truly stuck in the lock. She then became extremely considerate and her usual kind self and the incident was forgotten.

Next on the agenda was the Canadian National Exhibition, to take place in Toronto, followed by a tour of the Eastern States of the USA. The administrative officer designated to be in charge was the then Regimental Ad.-Maj. James Chichester Clarke, who was later appointed Prime Minister of Northern Ireland.

As we left Boston, Massachusetts and were crossing the Adirondack Mountains, Chichester Clarke said to Jaeger, 'Incidentally Jiggs, I received an invitation for some of the chaps, but it was too late. Some Count or other, sounded like some Polish chappie... aristocratic name... but aren't they all!' It came to light that Count Basie and his band had been playing Boston at the same time that we had been there and the world-famous band leader had extended an invitation to us via Chichester Clarke. And we missed it!

During the trip we made a guest appearance on the *Roy Rogers Show* complete with Trigger. Shades of Hell Fire Corner were not repeated as Trigger behaved impeccably.

It was not all work; some of us paid an off-duty visit to the restaurant and bar of the ex-heavyweight champion of the world, Jack Dempsey, where we were made most welcome. We were given coloured picture cards of the famous boxer fighting against Jess Willard in 1919, which had been autographed by Mr Dempsey.

Much of the time we followed in the path of Hurricane Hazel – which was not conducive to a successful tour – and we returned to the UK, flying back from Montreal on a Super Constellation.

JAMES MONTGOMERY FLAGG

JACK DEMPSEY KNOCKS OUT JESS WILLARD
TOLEDO, O. JULY 4, 1919 AND BECOMES
CHAMPION of the WORLD

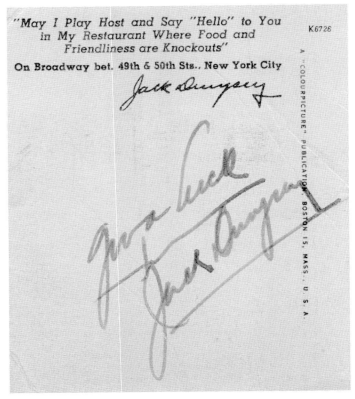

"May I Play Host and Say "Hello" to You
in My Restaurant Where Food and
Friendliness are Knockouts"

K 6726

On Broadway bet. 49th & 50th Sts., New York City

Jack Dempsey

A "COLOURPICTURE" PUBLICATION BOSTON 15, MASS., U.S.A.

Above: Postcard of Jack Dempsey.

Below: Jack Dempsey's autograph on the back of the postcard.

ten

The flying euphonium

Another of the Regimental Band's duties was playing at the Remembrance Service Ceremony, which took place in Whitehall each November. At a rehearsal of the massed bands on the square at Chelsea Barracks for one of these occasions, during a period of silence, there was a loud scream followed by a euphonium flying through the air. The missile landed about a yard from a rather bewildered mounted officer, who remained sitting motionless, as though nothing had occurred. The projector was none other than Pincher Martin, who had unfortunately suffered a mental breakdown.

After a rest at Nettley Military Hospital, Pincher was soon back in harness. Sadly, his euphonium had suffered more physical damage and took slightly longer to recuperate.

In 1955 Volkswagen celebrated the millionth production of the popular family car with a musical extravaganza, Viennese ballet, Cuban dancers, Band of the Danish Life Guards, French Naval Band and of course the Band of Her Majesty's Irish Guards. No expense was spared for the period of the event which lasted for three days in the town of Wolksburg, where the cars were produced. Apart from being well paid for their services, all participants were given a VW watch and a miniature 'beetle' car.

It was at this time that I was elevated to the heady ranks of lance corporal – a popular decision I thought, albeit not accepted by all. However, a most unpopular promotion was that of Sgt George Prior to band sergeant major. Out went first name terms and in came more discipline and political correctness. However, extremes of this nature are usually accompanied by characters who excel in the art of ridicule, and this was no exception. One such person was Les (Sailor) Dawkins, a horn player, who had transferred from the Royal Marines. Our illustrious new band sergeant would stand with his clipboard and pencil at readiness and bellow 'call the roll!' followed by the name of each bandsman, and each in turn would reply 'band sar'nt':

'Ainsworth.'
'Band sar'nt!'
'Bradbury.'
'Band sar'nt!'
'Dawkins.'
'Ba★★★★d!'

Licking his pencil and looking suspiciously in the direction of Dawkins, Sgt Prior would repeat 'Dawkins', to which the response this time would be 'band sar'nt!' Dawkins saved his face, but the band sergeant had been ridiculed, and this did not go unnoticed by Dawkins' fellow

Mounting guard at Buckingham Palace.

Volkswagen's millioneth car celebrations, 1955.

Jaeger and Nobby Clarke inspecting.

bandsmen. This act would be given time to rest for a period, before being repeated a month or so later, to the amusement of the bandsmen.

Another practical joke – which could have been a court martial offence – was played on 'Jiggs' Jaeger. Jaeger, whose name can be translated into German as 'Hunter', was an orphan and had been sent to join the King's Own Yorkshire Light Infantry as a boy. He excelled at Kneller Hall, the Military Musical Academy, being the youngest student ever to pass out from the Academy. From band master of the 4th Hussars, he had transferred to the Irish Guards as a captain and was full of personality – he was a charismatic and brilliant showman, although his conducting was sometimes susceptible. He was extremely popular, especially with the royal household!

Early one hot summer morning 'someone' went into Jiggs' room at Chelsea, before his batman had arrived. A full tin of Kiwi Black boot polish was emptied into the inside of Jiggs' bearskin, the last piece of dress put on before going on parade.

The regiment proceeded to march towards Buck House while all the time the boot polish melted in the hot sunshine and spread all over Jiggs' face, much to the amusement of all concerned. Jiggs' seemed to be unaware that his facial colour was changing and it was only on his return to barracks, enjoying a gin and tonic in the officers' mess, that he was he made aware of his embarrassing situation. A serious interrogation took place within the band personnel, but the culprit was never found. Or was he?

On occasions there would be a massed band concert given at Kneller Hall for the students, normally held in an outside auditorium having the resemblance of a Roman amphitheatre. We played in normal uniform forage caps during the performances – the bearskins had to be kept on one side for the National Anthem, which was played at the end of each performance. This gave an ideal opportunity for the beer drinkers, who would be seated behind the poor unsuspecting woodwind players, diligently engaged and completely unaware of their forthcoming fate until Lt. Col Sam Rhodes, senior director of music, would shout in his broad Rochdale dialect, 'Burrskin caps on… The Queen'. What was to happen to the unsuspecting woodwind players leaves little to the imagination!

There were some unsavoury things which sadly were a part of regimental life. On one occasion, being in charge of the 'kit party' and the last to leave the palace, we entered the Wellington Barracks and the then duty sergeant caught my eye, being the last to enter the barracks. He invited me to return after dismissal of the party on the promise of a surprise. As I returned I witnessed a young drummer lad leaving the guard room fastening his trouser buttons. 'Help yourself,' said the Sergeant motioning towards the cell. 'A regimental captain of noble birth has just been in there'.

I was physically sick when I saw the scene inside the cell and declined the Sergeant's invitation to participate. I left the scene thinking of the price some wretched people were prepared to pay for a bed or a meal.

Another disturbing incident took place at Satan Camp in Cheshire, where we were stationed for a week, ostensibly for parade ground activities at Eaton Hall. Eaton Hall was situated in beautiful grounds and was used as a centre for the training of National Service Officers.

I required a dentist and reported to the guard room where I was told that if I reported on the following morning I could get lift, as there was a party accompanying a dangerous prisoner into Chester at that time. When I arrived early that morning the iron door to the cell opened and at first it appeared that the cell was empty. The stench that met my nostrils was appalling and I noticed a small naked figure sitting on a bed surrounded by a pile of dirty plates. When he came into the light I could see that his body and his face were covered in bruises; he had obviously been very badly beaten. He was guilty of refusing to soldier in any way or form and this was his punishment. He was forcibly dressed and dragged out in between two corporals, each carrying rifles.

The poor unfortunate was on his way to Shepton Mallet, an Army detention centre, and was sitting between the two corporals in the back of an Army Champ, all the time staring at me as if

A photograph taken by Kenny Pinches shortly before he died.

to plead for help. He did not appear to have the strength even to stand unaided and I felt utterly helpless and useless. Whatever happened to him I shall never know, but the place he was being taken from would be heaven, compared to his destination!

It was not unusual for eminent officers to pay casual visits to the band rehearsals and on several occasions we were visited by Bde. J.O.E. Vandeleur, Irish Guards, who led the Guards Armoured Division on their way to relieve the troops at Arnhem. In the film *A Bridge Too Far* the part of Bde. Vandeleur was played by Michael Caine.

St Patrick's Day was always a special event for us 'Micks'. The Queen Mother, who had a special affection for the regiment, would occasionally present shamrocks on this special day. If the regiment were dressed in khaki, the shamrock would be worn behind the cap star of the forage cap. Should the regiment be in ceremonial attire the shamrock would be tucked into the curb chain of the bearskin. The RSM would then bellow 'remove headdress!', followed by, 'three cheers for Her Majesty!' The inevitable march-past would take place to the regimental quick march *Paddy's Day* and was followed by libations in the mess, quite often leading to high-spirited pranks.

It was the Micks' band's turn for a short tour of duty with the Fourth Guards Brigade in Germany. The First Grenadiers and Second Scots Guards were to be stationed at Hubelrath. A few miles outside of the city of Düsseldorf and situated in beautiful surroundings, the barracks were modern, with leafy avenues, and had been built just before the Second World War especially for the SS.

We embarked at Harwich for the overnight crossing to the Hook of Holland, sailing on the *Empire Parkstone*, an old, antiquated iron tub. Introduced to our quarters, lower ranks found themselves in the bowels of the boat with three-tiered bunks on each side of a narrow gangway which led to a small wash room and toilet. Securing all our equipment we settled down to what appeared to be a reasonably quiet and peaceful crossing.

Just before the journey began at 11.45 p.m. the unexpected happened and a nightmare scenario was unfolded. Down came the Black Watch into the already cramped sleeping area and although whisky was in abundance, it did not improve matters. The crossing was rough, the ship was heaving and most of us were ill. The toilet became blocked, sending the refuse down the gangway into the sleeping area. Those who were fortunate enough to get some sleep were constantly interrupted by a kilt wafting overhead.

Thankfully we were assembled on deck in the fresh air on arrival and although the weather was still atrocious and we stood in pouring rain it was still a relief to escape the night's horrors. We had all been soaked to the skin waiting for disembarkation and it was a further relief to board the train to make our way to Düsseldorf.

Although the barracks were beautifully situated, most of the area was surrounded by a high wire fence. Behind the hut where we found ourselves accommodated was a conveniently cut escape hatch, which had been introduced by a long-serving inmate when a curfew was still in existence curtailing any late-night revels. The secret entrance, as it transpired, was vital to our existence after an enjoyable evening in the nearby village of Rattingen. About 3.00 a.m. the sound of heavy boots could be heard in the corridor outside our room. This was followed by a very large sergeant in the Queen's Company, who told us to get dressed and to form outside on the square. I thought I was dreaming, but no, it was really happening! Not expecting to be long on parade I put my khaki and blue cape over my pyjamas.

The rain was torrential as we formed up in the middle of the square, which at the time was lined with Army trucks full of sleeping soldiers of the First Battalion Grenadiers on their way to the City of Bruges to be presented with the Freedom of the City. When the RSM eventually gave the order for the trucks to move we must have played The British Grenadiers at least a thousand times and we were all soaked to the skin. We were up at 6.00 a.m. for breakfast wearing wet sodden khaki after which we boarded trucks to be driven to Nuremberg for a rehearsal for a tattoo.

After a month had passed our tour of duty came to an end and we returned to the UK on the ship *Vienna,* which, it was rumoured, had seen service in the Crimean War. There was only one casualty throughout our time in Germany: a trombone player and respected member of the Salvation Army had to be left behind, suffering from the effects of an illicit liaison with a local friendly Fraulein.

Extra rehearsals, Chelsea Barracks, 1954.

Roger Rostron, myself and Ted Cullen at our reunion in 2004.

eleven

Oh Danny Boy…
shades of Northern Ireland

One morning, standing under the arch at Wellington Barracks sorting out my marches and preparing to go on 'guard mounting', I was confronted by a stranger asking me if my name was Casson. It seemed that the young lad who was with the Black Watch had just arrived from Kneller Hall on transfer to the Irish Guards and had been told to ask for me, bringing best wishes from Peter Hey, my friend from way back in the Queensbury band. That very moment Jiggs Jaeger arrived, together with one other officer, the RSM and two corporals. The young stranger was stood to attention with bayonet drawn and was instructed to produce his clarinet for its number. On producing his instrument he was immediately taken to the guard room, marching between the two corporals.

It is a well-known fact in the musical world that clarinets are like magpies and come in twos; B flat and A. When the young stranger produced only one instrument he was immediately under suspicion as two clarinets had gone missing from Kneller Hall. The question was, where was the other?

Through sheer coincidence about one month later I was walking down Victoria Street when who should I bump into but Mr Kenealy, the old 'trained soldier' from the Guards depot at Caterham. After passing the time of day he asked me if I knew of anyone who wanted to buy a clarinet in excellent condition. My surprise at his knowledge of how the instrument came to be in his possession added to the mystery of whatever happened to the Black Watch musician last seen being marched off to the guard room… no doubt he would have enjoyed his time in the Shepton Mallet Ensemble!

Windsor Castle was a summer duty for a Regimental Band whenever the Queen was in residence, each regiment taking its turn at the duty. The usual daily Changing of the Guard up and down the cobbled hill and onto the green; Sunday afternoons on the terrace only yards from the royals taking their afternoon tea – the programme having been already presented to them for their approval. I always imagined the Order of the Bath coming my way, as I cannot recall how many times I have played *Danny Boy* for the Queen Mother. A wave perhaps, a smile… but nothing, not even a bath bun; all part of the duty!

Recruiting tours were a more gentle way of attracting candidates without the impersonal National Service 'invitation'. Most of the time these were monotonous expeditions spent hanging round windswept corners in Hollywood Barracks, Armagh and one time in a small RAF camp at Cannock Chase near Birmingham. Pincher Martin's birthday was celebrated in the local pub, after which we continued on to the green of the barracks. The RAF police,

Inspection on Guard Mounting Ceremony, Wellington Barracks.

having declined our invitation to join the birthday celebrations, reciprocated by inviting us into their cells for the remainder of the evening. In the early hours of the following day the by now familiar iron doors of the cell were opened and we stumbled into the daylight at 6.00 a.m. just in time for Paddy Donnelly's early morning tea.

A more unusual way of entertainment was provided by the Scots Guards Band on recruiting tours and tattoos known as 'Putting the Soap'. Standing in their khaki shirts they would each in turn place a large piece of carbolic soap, tapered at the end, in between their buttocks. The ultimate objective of this exercise was to project the piece of carbolic soap with as much force as possible to see who could reach the furthest point. The latest recruit was given the title of 'The Chalk Man' and would be responsible for the distance mark. The champion at that time was Geordie Braithwaite, who had the powerful projection to reach half way up the opposite wall, which sometimes proved too difficult for The Chalk Man to reach!

In the summer of 1957, as the seventeen members of the concert band formed a circle in a makeshift jungle in Elstree Studios, we were aware of a small stout gentleman waiting to conduct us, not in playing our instruments but in whistling. The gentleman was Malcolm Arnold, who had written the music for the film *Bridge on the River Kwai,* and we had been seconded to whistle the tune *Colonel Bogey*, which was part of the soundtrack as the British prisoners came out of the jungle. Arnold had the habit of walking up to individuals during recording and pulling faces, which inevitably caused lots of breakdowns.

Eventually they decided on an acceptable take and the band was asked to play at the première of the film, which was shown at the Marble Arch Odeon. My whistling prowess earned me the

My parents watching the Irish Guards leaving Windsor Castle.

princely sum of £6. Imagine how many times that tune has been heard around the world since that day!

A sixteen-week world tour had been arranged for the band, pipes and drums of the First Battalion Irish Guards. In overall charge of the operation was a regimental fanatic, Maj. John Head, Irish Guards, Independent Parachute Company, and none too popular. He was unapproachable; should a need arise the only way was through the band sergeant pipe or drum major. His brother, Anthony, held the position of Minister of War at that time.

After the usual afternoon and evening concerts at the Canadian National Exhibition in Toronto, our second visit, the late-night entertainment was provided at the Armouries. There, in the different messes of the Canadian Black Watch, Grenadiers and Princess Patricia's Light Infantry, were the inevitable drinking contests.

It was not uncommon and more likely for a saffron-kilted, bare-chested piper to be seen standing on top of a table with a Canadian for the 'final challenge'. One afternoon Jiggs announced to the audience that the Canadian Air Force had given us a new arrangement of a musical which had recently opened in New York. After ploughing our way through the piece, Jiggs held his nose and threw the score over his shoulder into the audience, which met with rapturous applause – the musical in question being *My Fair Lady*!

Next stop Los Angeles and a concert at the Shrine Auditorium, Hollywood USA. Pitch black and deadly silent, it appeared to be empty until I walked down a ramp leading from the stage to play my cornet solo. To my amazement there was an abundance of stars sitting in the audience only a few feet away from where I was to play: Betty Hutton, Doris Day, Rock Hudson, Rory Calhoun and Jack Palance, to name but a few of the famous faces staring in admiration.

During the interval, the British actor Anthony Steele, an ex-Grenadier officer himself, and friend of John Head, was anxiously trying to rescue his new wife, Anita Ekberg, from the claws of several drummers.

The following evening, together with Pat Purcell (one of my closest friends in the band at the time), we were invited to the Blue Gardenia Night Club in Wiltshire Boulevard. Our American friends spotted Louella Parsons, the famous gossip columnist, and a film producer leaving the club together. After being introduced to them the film producer invited Pat and myself to the MGM studios for a film test as he was looking for a couple of English guys for a small part in a film he was making. It would mean that we would have to desert the British Army, we explained. 'Then desert, God Damn it!' was his reply. It wasn't to be – the thought of a court martial was too daunting – and so it was breakfast at Googies, Downtown LA at 4.00 a.m. and onwards to Honolulu.

During the visit there was an interview with Maj. Head, who you will remember was the brother of the then Minister of War, by a reporter from the *Los Angeles Echo*. When asked for the British Army's reaction on the recent H bomb tests done by the British, Maj Head's response was that the only answer to the H bomb was a rifle and bayonet!

On arrival at Honolulu we were greeted by a bevy of beautiful dusky Hawaiian maidens waiting to present us with the traditional garlands. With no concerts planned for a few days we stayed at the Reef and Edge Water hotels, enjoying the balmy evenings, dancing under the stars and palm trees of the internationally well-known Mowana Club… we had arrived! What would they be doing back in Queensbury? Horace and Dirty Old Bill still groping up June's skirt no doubt! All thoughts that went through my head as I lay on Waikiki Beach watching the surfers.

The United States Marine Band invited a few of us over to Schofield Barracks which had featured in the steamy scenes in the film *From Here to Eternity*, then a moving and memorable visit to the memorial site at Pearl Harbour.

Onward throughout the tour it had become noticeable that some members of the band were losing money; it would seem there was a thief in the band. After a short stopover calling in a bamboo hut in Fiji Airport, we landed in Sydney, New South Wales. Our home for the next two weeks would be a hotel on Bondi beach and the venue for the concerts was the Old Tivoli Theatre, built in the late nineteenth century.

During the concerts the absence of a piper was noted; his sexuality had been in question for some time, but as he had a close working relationship with Maj. Head no further questions had been asked… but we all had our own suspicions who the tea leaf was.

twelve

Tours 'down under'

Parties seemed to be the norm 'down under'. There was a young woman working in the theatre as an usherette and I invited her to come along to one of the many that were to be held on Bondi beach. She agreed to come to the party providing that she could stay to the end of the concert as she wanted to hear a young 'English' singer perform; that young singer was no other than Welsh-born Shirley Bassey!

At another party which was given by the Bondi Beach Life Savers, a well-oiled 'Aussie' asked me if I was the solo 'trumpeter' with the Guards, as he had just bought a new trumpet and wanted me to give it a try out. Although it was very late by this time a few of us agreed to accompany him to his house, where there was more alcohol in the form of 'tinnies' (Australian six-packs). While one of us looked after the sausages (!) another took care of the booze and I was left with our guest, who put this brand new Busher Trumpet into my hands. 'Blow it as loud as you can mate,' was the instruction, and I did – obviously not loud enough for his taste, as he demanded that I blew it even louder. At this point I became dizzy with the effects of the alcoholic consumption of the evening and the oxygen going to my head… I stumbled against a table where I had laid the trumpet. Unbeknownst to us, the wife of our guest, who had been sleeping soundly, entered the room, picked up the trumpet and unceremoniously bashed me over the head with said trumpet.

Before we left Sydney, a few of us were invited to an arts ball, which took place in a ballroom, the largest in the Antipodes. As we did not posses any fancy dress, our Australian friends suggested that we should attend the ball in our Blue Patrol uniforms, not forgetting the obligatory 'tinnies'.

At some time during the evening's festivities, enjoying our 'grog', we were approached by a scantily-dressed gorgeous blonde, who proceeded to sit on the knee of Pat Purcell, my companion of possible future film-star status in LA. It did not take too much 'amore' to persuade Pat to take to the already heaving dance floor with the blonde. Obviously it was love at first sight for Pat and hands began to feverishly explore, which were expertly guided by the blonde towards the lower regions! The first shock for Pat was, 'Don't you remember me, Pat?' This was followed by what Pat discovered in the lower regions – what he found belonging to Wally, the blond barman from Wallongong, who had entertained us all in his pub some three weeks earlier. Pat had obviously made a big impression.

An old steam train would puff its way down the main dusty street of Port Pirie and the local sheep shearers' horses were tied to the bars outside the various refreshment emporiums. After a

Entertaining Adelaide school children, South Australia.

concert which had been held in a nearby field, I was fortunate to be chosen by a few 'Sheilas' to accompany them to a party which was being held at a farmhouse. The farm was at the end of a seven-mile long straight road leading into the bush.

After a few beers I decided it was time to go 'scouting' and I soon realised there was an uneven distribution of talent at the party. Not wishing to intrude on already established liaisons and feeling rather lonely, I thought it best to make my way home… but how? I started the seven-mile hike in pitch blackness broken only by the stars, counting the telegraph poles and avoiding the dead wombats in the road. A few miles down the dusty road I saw a light in the distance. After some time I could distinguish two lights which to my delight turned into the shape of an open-topped old Morris 8 motorcar. The driver was from Scotland and well inebriated. His companion sharing the front seat was a half-consumed bottle of an amber coloured liquid. In his broad native accent, which I found difficult to understand, he seemed to be enquiring as to what the hell was I doing out there. I told him I was making my way back to Port Pirie. 'Jump in,' he said, and very kindly turned the car around and drove the next five miles or so, where I thanked him graciously for the lift and the 'spirit' in which he had helped me.

One hot steamy morning at the bottom of a hill in Brisbane, formed up in full dress uniform, were four 'volunteered' musicians: a young drummer boy carrying a wreath, and pipe and drum majors, under the charge of the ever-present Maj. Head. The major began to explain the morning's serious procedure. We were to march up the hill to the Cenotaph, where there would be two Australian private soldiers standing at ease. When approached, the 'Aussies' were expected to come to attention, slope and present arms. The major would then lay the wreath on the Cenotaph.

What really happened was, as we reached the Cenotaph, coming to a halt, the major was greeted in a friendly fashion by one of the Aussie soldiers: 'G'day major! F★★★ing hot t'day ain't it?' – ignoring the drill routine and never moving from being 'at ease'! We 'about turned' and retired to the bottom of the hill, suppressing our humour with difficulty.

We all missed our families, girlfriends and wives during the long tour of duty in the lower hemisphere, but there were occasions when the enforced celibacy of the Guards was in dispute. During our stay in Melbourne one 'lady of the night' (who earned the title of the 'Melbourne Muncher') could be found on the back seat of one of the band buses, performing her duties. A certain drum major, upon enquiring what was the commotion taking place at the back of the bus, expressed his disgust when the reasons for the jollity became evident. It was therefore surprising to find the same gentleman in a similar position one evening – but even more surprising and amusing to note the gentleman in question was still holding his ceremonial mace.

thirteen

A scholarship and the Royal College of Music

Leaving Australia behind and heading for home we had a stopover in Karachi when the plane was delayed from take off as an angry Indian souk dealer made accusations against the company, as one of his expensive fez hats appeared to be missing. It seemed that no one on board was responsible and the plane was allowed to take off. Later in the flight a bare-chested piper wearing only his saffron kilt serenaded the passengers, playing his pipes and sporting a very smart fez!

We found ourselves grounded in Rome due to heavy fog, where the airline company accommodated us in excellent five-star accommodation in the centre of the city. About to leave the hotel and take in the sights of Rome, we were alerted to a dramatic and strong argument taking place in the hotel reception between the hotel manager and John Derek, the American film star, along with his girlfriend, the young Ursula Andress of future Bond fame. One of our party, notorious for his amorous and personal introductions to the female sex, addressed Miss Andress directly: 'If you don't like your room darling, you can come and stay with me!' – upon which John Derek became even more irate, grabbing his lady friend by the arm and leaving the hotel.

The tour had been interesting in more ways than one, but here we were back in Blighty and to routine duties. Some of the lighter moments breaking the sometimes monotonous duties were visits to the Royal College of Music in South Kensington. Here we were to be conducted by military students from Kneller Hall as this was a part of their training and studies for their ARCM qualifications.

Ernest Hall, professor of trumpet and retired principal trumpet of the BBC Symphony Orchestra, asked me if I had ever thought of becoming a student at the college. Of course I was flattered by his interest, but had to admit I did not have the money to attend the college. Professor Hall explained that there was such a thing as an Army Scholarship, which would pay for one year's tuition as a student for a successful candidate.

This idea appealed to me and after much consideration I decided to apply for an interview with then principal of the Royal College, Sir Ernest Bullock, who, being an ex-military man himself, was most sympathetic to my situation. It was arranged for me to have an audition, which was a successful one, as two weeks later I received a formal invitation to study trumpet with Ernest Hall at the Royal College. And so I began the rather bizarre existence for twelve months of 'playing at soldiers' for a part of the day and being a 'student of trumpet' for the remainder. There was not much chance to earn extra money doing gigs – I was hard up but happy.

Earnest Hall showing his wife the miniature trumpet.

It became quite apparent to me that in life it's who you know and not always what you know that gets you on, and this was the case in my newly acquired musical career.

Immediately after I started my tuition with Professor Hall, he introduced me to Frank Smith, the trombone professor and then orchestral manager at Covent Garden Opera House. This led to many off-stage engagements at the Opera House, such as *Meistersinger* and *Aida,* during the next three years.

Meanwhile, back at the band I found myself taking part in a live BBC production of *Friday Night is Music Night.* Just as I was about to start playing the solo 'Zelda' in front of the usual audience, the middle valve spring of my cornet snapped! My colleague Tom Merry threw me his cornet and I was able to play the solo somewhat shakily! A week later I received a letter in the post from my old mentor, William Arthur Lang. 'You pinched my Zelda,' wrote Willie; 'best of luck'. Bill, who had heard the programme, was now principal trumpet with the Halle Orchestra, based in Manchester. Not bad for a stonemason and Army tank driver!

fourteen

Love and marriage

I had some girlfriends and associates, but never anything too serious – not enough time in my life. However, during the tour of Australia I had been shown a photograph of a particularly pretty dark-haired girlfriend of a trombone player, Mike Biddulph. Mike's girlfriend was a student violinist at the Royal College of Music. Mike was tragically killed following a motorcycle accident and one of the saddest moments of my life was when I acted as a pall-bearer when he was given a military funeral.

I met the dark-haired young lady whose photograph Mike had proudly shown me at Mike's funeral and later I became friendly with Jill. The friendship blossomed and we became engaged and were married, going on to live in married quarters at Wallington, Surrey.

I kept a close contact with Mike's parents, and David, his father (also a trombone player, albeit amateur), formed the London Gabrielle Brass Ensemble. I would sometimes accompany David as he carried out his work as a sales director. This led to meeting 'interesting' people such as 'Nick the Greek' and Ronnie Kray, one of the Kray Brothers. Both notorious gangsters at the time, I always found them charming company and it was hard to imagine the lives they were reputed to live.

There were many up-and-coming stars studying at the Royal College. Jimmy Galway, later to be knighted Sir James, and Gwynneth Jones, later to be Dame Gwynneth, the Wagnerian Diva, were just a couple.

Professor Ernest Hall seemed to spend more time regaling me with his tales of life in the Army, instead of teaching the trumpet, and yet I gained so much knowledge about the classical side of trumpet playing from him. One of his stories was when Ernest had served in the Liverpool Regiment during the First World War. He was one of the unfortunates who had been stood in the trenches all night long waiting to 'go over the top' at the Somme the following morning. He often recalled how on that day, shortly before the whistle blew to 'go over the top', a rather nervous young man indulged him in conversation during which Ernest told the lad that he had been a student of trumpet at the RCM. Then over they went together. Ernest fell wounded into a shell hole, never to see his recently acquired friend again.

In 1929, after broadcasting the Haydn Trumpet Concerto with the Queens Hall Orchestra, Ernest received a letter postmarked Montreal, Canada. In the letter was written, 'I heard a trumpet concerto played on the radio and wonder if you could be the person who stood alongside me in the trench on the Somme in July 1916?'

As you can tell, I have my share of memories. One of those is of sitting in an ashtray (sorry, box) at the Royal Albert Hall as one of the offstage trumpets in Berlioz's *Grande Messe des Morts,* playing with the Royal Philharmonic Orchestra. Sitting next to me was a long-serving member of the trumpet fraternity whose name was Bert Barr. He pointed to the conductor saying, 'that young lad is two years younger than I am'. This happened very shortly before the death of the 'young conductor' – none other than Sir Thomas Beecham.

There were ninety-eight rehearsal rooms in the Royal College of Music and I was having a pint of local tipple in the ninety-nineth (a bar around the corner) with the chief administrator of the college, Percy Showan, who was responsible for room allocations. I confessed to Percy that I had completed my year's Army Scholarship, to which he replied, 'if they [the Army] are paying, keep blowing and say nothing'. So I did and completed another year at the RCM.

After a second year in college and a successful freelance career which had developed in and around London, I received a letter from the principal trumpet of the City of Birmingham Symphony Orchestra, Bram Gay, who originally had been a celebrated solo cornet player with the Foden's Motorworks Brass Band.

He was writing to me concerning a vacancy which he knew was about to arise as second trumpet in his orchestra. Would I be interested in taking an audition? It was patently obvious that my intentions were to move on in my career and it was becoming increasingly difficult for me to take any time off from the Guards Band. So, what was I to do? I still had several months left to serve out my time and it was not going to be an easy time. An appointment to discuss my position with the CO was not successful, as he had already been made aware of my intentions. The importance of my contribution in the forthcoming Trooping that year was stressed.

I had to inform the City of Birmingham Symphony Orchestra of my situation, but they could only hold the position open for one month. It suddenly occurred to me that the Revd Gentleman, who had performed at my wedding, had at one time been a chaplain to the Forces… perhaps a letter from him would do the trick. It seems that I had a trump card up my sleeve and I played an ace.

There was £120 sitting in my Post Office account and this was the exact amount required for me to buy my release from the Army. This left me completely broke, not a penny in the world and a baby on the way.

And so another chapter in my life came to a close. I left the military behind with memories of some of the greatest characters, and pals I shall never forget. Sad also to be leaving London, but the prospect of regular work and income was more inviting than the rat-race of 'town', as it was known.

Next stop Birmingham to join the orchestra and to accept an additional offer from the principal of the Birmingham School of Music, Sir Stewart Wilson, to teach at the college.

fifteen

Experiences in the City of Birmingham Symphony Orchestra

Ernest Parsons had been the timpanist in the City of Birmingham Symphony Orchestra (CBSO) for many years. Small, white haired, slightly eccentric and constantly chain smoking, Ernie became a father figure. He delighted in showing a photograph of himself as a liaison officer on a camel alongside Lawrence of Arabia, and was known to have stormed out of a performance of the film.

One morning, during a rehearsal taken by Meredith Davies, there was a loud and unexpected rumble from the 'tymps'. 'What is this orchestra coming to, where are the true Britons? There has no' been a mention of the British War Dead. I demand a two minute silence; it's the eleventh'. Meredith turned to Meyer Stolow, the leader, and suggested that we comply with Ernie's wishes! 'Ladies and Gentlemen, would you please stand for two minutes silence,' he requested. After about a minute and half, Stan Smith, a member of the first violins, quietly said to Meredith, 'Excuse me Mr Davies, but it is only the tenth today!' The whole orchestra burst into laughter, much to the embarrassment of poor old Ernie.

Sir Adrian Boult, rehearsing with the orchestra for a concert of English music that contained an arrangement by Beecham, was interrupted by Meyer Stolow with one of his many suggestions. Sir Adrian's response was 'Mr Stolow! [Sir Adrian was always very polite in addressing the members of the orchestra] I appreciate your suggestions, but I don't think it advisable to play around too much with Sir Thomas's private parts!'

Maggie Cotton, a member of the percussion section who was noted for being rather flat-chested, was responsible for the cymbal part in the Holst Planets Suite during another rehearsal. Sir Adrian, fingering his well-groomed moustache, politely requested 'more sound from the cymbals'. Maggie tried to oblige and gave the cymbals another CRASH! 'My dear young lady,' said Sir Adrian, 'is that the largest pair in Birmingham?'

A very well-respected drummer who on occasions came up to Birmingham from London to play with the CBSO was a dapper gentleman, but a little on the short side and was also Canadian. At one rehearsal he found himself standing behind a particularly large drum which was required as part of the score of Vaughan Williams' *Antarctica Symphony*. Once again Sir Adrian was asking for more sound; 'Hello, are you there?' Not being able to see the rather diminutive drummer, he turned to the leader of the orchestra asking, 'Does he work on Saturdays?'

Harold Grey had been an associate conductor with the CBSO for a number of years, always stepping into the breach in times of emergency. After a week of Mahler with Jascha Horenstein, schools concerts in the Town Hall came as a light relief. 'Good afternoon boys and girls,' said

The City of Birmingham Symphony Orchestra.

Harold; 'I'm sure you are all familiar with the major works of Sibelius,' was one of his reputed *faux pas*. Another was, 'I can see you are all becoming agitated, so we are going to play you a very soothing piece by Bach called…' then, turning around, as he had momentarily forgotten the title, he said '… Sheep… May… Graze… Securely' in a very strong Brummie accent.

Graham Lacey, playing second trombone, had previously worked in the orchestra pit at the Birmingham Hippodrome. 'I have been here too long now,' said the old trombone player sitting next to Graham. 'I get fed up, night after night… but where do I go?' At that moment the old man took out a penknife from his pocket and thrust the knife into his leg. Lacey turned white, expecting a spurt of blood from a severed artery from the old man's leg and watching nervously as the old man continued to play his trombone with the knife sticking out of his leg – his wooden leg!

The Welsh National Opera had no professional orchestra at that time and would hire the CBSO for their opera season. Performing *Tosca* in Llandudno with Joan Sutherland and Roland Jones, a request was made of Roland from one member of the brass section. 'Why don't you give us a euphonium solo?' And surprisingly, just before the tea break, on to the stage walked Roland playing his euphonium. Originally from Gwancaergurwen in South Wales, Roland had been Black Dyke's principal euphonium player before the Second World War and would usually sing his encore. After hearing him sing someone suggested that he should study singing and he did – becoming a principal tenor at Sadler's Wells.

Bram Gay, a most polished professional and methodical trumpet player, was showing interest in the principal trumpet position with the London Symphony Orchestra. He had been invited to play in two concerts with this orchestra in the Royal Festival Hall, London. The CBSO management however refused permission for time off, so Bram produced a 'sick note' – an extremely clever move in the form of political assassination followed with a letter to the CBSO from an alleged Birmingham business man. 'As a staunch CBSO supporter on a visit to London,' read the letter, 'I attended a concert at the Festival Hall and was thrilled see our very own principal trumpet player taking part... ' Obviously this was all planned and the culprit vanished into the fog of the London scene. Fortunately the Halle Orchestra first chair position was available and Bram left the CBSO to occupy the vacancy in the Halle. It was musical chairs time again, for who went to the LSO instead of Bram but... William Arthur Lang.

Jack Pinches, one of the brothers from the Black Dyke Band and now playing with the BBC Symphony Orchestra, invited Bill Lang to do some teaching at Eton School. Bill was about to go on tour to Daytona Beach and asked the music master at Eton if he should make up the lost time before or after the tour. 'Don't worry... use your own judgment,' came the reply. A week later a letter arrived from the headmaster of Eton School insisting that Bill should decide where his allegiance lay; the orchestra or the school. What followed is the famous telegram...
'STICK JOB UP ARSE... RUDE LETTER TO FOLLOW!'

sixteen

Britten's War Requiem, Coventry Cathedral, 1963

All masterpieces have to have a first performance and yet most first performances are not masterpieces. Most professional orchestras are aware of this in promoting the cause of new music. However, it became an exceptional source of anticipation when the CBSO came to play its part in unleashing Benjamin Britten's *War Requiem* on an unsuspecting world.

The *War Requiem* was composed for the consecration of the rebuilt Coventry Cathedral and, like the cathedral, was conceived as a symbol of reconciliation seventeen years after the end of the Second World War.

Its three solo parts were assigned to Galina Vishnevskaya, Peter Pears and Dietrich Fischer Dieskau, representing Russia, Great Britain and Germany. The Soviet government refused to allow Vishnevskaya to travel outside of Russia and the soprano part at the first performance was sung by Heather Harper, whose sister Alison was a member of the CBSO cello section at that time.

It was an exceptionally difficult piece, especially when reading it for the first time, coupled with the poor acoustics in the cathedral. A further problem that became apparent during the rehearsals was that the workers were still dismantling the scaffolding, which led to a great amount of background noise. Three conductors were required, with Britten himself directing the Melos Ensemble in the Wilfred Owen settings, Meredith Davies conducting the choir and orchestra and David Lepine in charge of the young boy choristers.

Britten called a percussion and brass sectional rehearsal, then concentrated on the exposed and difficult trumpet fanfares. When it came to the first performance (there were actually two 'first' performances), Britten had requested that there should be no applause and at the end of the performance there was a deathly silence, probably lasting as long as two minutes, and no one seemed to know what to do. There was no doubt that anyone having taken part in such a moving performance would never forget the evening.

Soon after the event Hugo Rignold became principal conductor of the CBSO. Hugo was French Canadian and was always accompanied by his daughter Jennifer, a beautiful ex ballerina at Covent Garden 'rediscovered' by her father during a ballet performance when he was conducting from the orchestra pit.

As conductor of the orchestra, Hugo Rignold was positioned some distance away from the woodwind and brass, so he adopted the habit of asking for any questions to be repeated. During a rehearsal at Cheltenham Town Hall, Frank Allen – the newly appointed bass clarinet – asked Rignold in his broad Black Country accent if he could tell him what his second note in the

The rehearsal at Coventry Cathedral for the first performance of Britten's *War Requiem*.

third bar of section B was. As was the norm with this conductor, he asked the clarinetist to repeat the question, but still did not understand… so turning to John Geordiadis, the then leader, he asked, 'What did he say, John?'

'He wants to know if you will give him a lift back to Brum after the concert!' was the response.

During a three week tour of Germany the orchestra gave a performance of Beethoven in an old Luftwaffe airplane hangar on the outskirts of Nuremburg. An eighty-three-year-old white-haired lady, Proffessor Elly Ney of the University of Nuremburg, was the piano soloist in Beethoven´s *Emperor Concerto*. This lady was, reputedly, a favourite pianist of Hitler and was banned from leaving East Germany. No performance since has ever compared with such brilliance. It is very sad that, unfortunately, Elly Ney never made any recordings for posterity.

Sir Stewart Wilson's administrations at the Birmingham School of Music always created a relaxed and happy atmosphere, where students would mix freely and share the same dining tables as their tutors. Sir Stewart and Sir Adrian had earlier exchanged wives, Lady Wilson becoming Lady Boult and vice versa! The new principal appointed to take over as director of the school was Gordon Clinton of the 'Clinton Singers', whose attitude towards administration would change the atmosphere in the school dramatically: Clinton had no love for the CBSO and began to systematically remove any teacher who had connections or played with the orchestra.

The CBSO brass section, Worcester Cathedral, 1963.

This left John Fuest, principal clarinet, and myself. It was of little consequence to John as he was soon to move on and join the Royal Liverpool Philharmonic, so I was left stranded.

A cricket match had been arranged at the Cadbury's Cricket Ground between the CBSO and the Birmingham School of Music. As I was a fairly good bowler, Clinton had requested and then insisted that I should play for the School of Music. Declining the 'offer', I explained that I always played for the CBSO and had no intentions of doing otherwise on this occasion. The match took place on a beautiful summer day and the School of Music went in to bat, led by Clinton wearing his college cap complete with tassel. Taking his time at the crease and looking around, Clinton prepared himself to take the first delivery from the fast bowler... me! With the first delivery I took off his bails and everyone cheered, including his students, as he dejectedly walked back to the pavilion, leaving me with a distinct feeling of insecurity... This was the beginning of the end of my time at the Birmingham School of Music.

It was not long before Clinton appointed a young, inexperienced trumpet teacher from Huddersfield to join the school as trumpet tutor, thus jeopardising my own position. During a meeting with Clinton I told him that I was unable to be subservient to an amateur brass teacher of no repute. 'So your resignation will be accepted then,' was his reply, continuing, 'of course you will be required to fulfil the three months which is agreed in your contract'. I was not at all surprised by the way I was being treated and was prepared, having previously been for an audition with BBC Northern Symphony Orchestra. With the knowledge that there was a position for me in this orchestra, should I want to accept it, I told Mr Clinton that if he could find a contract, he knew what he could do with it! I then turned on my heel and left.

seventeen

BBC Northern Symphony Orchestra

Just before I made my dramatic exit from BSM we had had a visit from George Hurst, at the time the conductor of the BBC Northern Symphony Orchestra. Knowing that an old friend of mine from my Queensbury days with the Black Dyke, Maurice Murphy, had recently joined the BBC Northern Symphony Orchestra as principal trumpet, I asked George how Maurice was getting on. 'I can't kill that guy,' said George in admiration and jest... So I looked forward with great anticipation to rejoining Maurice and many of my old friends, as well as a chance to return to my native Northern lands!

I was not too surprised to bump into Jim Pope again. This time Jim had progressed his career to the height of sound engineer working in Manchester. These meetings were becoming something of a regular joke!

This was a time before the new BBC Centre had been built in Oxford Street, Manchester, and different departments were scattered across the city. The Milton Hall in Deansgate, Manchester was the home of the orchestra and next door to 'The Grapes', a public house frequented by the actors of *Coronation Street* and other programmes. When broadcasting on a Sunday, Maurice and I would walk up to the studios in Piccadilly for lunch and a game of snooker, where the table was occupied, more often than not, by little Jimmy Clitheroe and his producer, Jimmy Casey. Casey's father was the famous comedian Jimmy James.

Maurice would throw down the gauntlet and take the two of them on in a foursome, whispering to me, 'Let me go before little Jimmy!' as after every shot he would leave the white cue ball in the centre of the full-sized snooker table and of course Jimmy had no chance of reaching it, especially using his own small cue. Jimmy would respond in his Lancashire accent, 'Eeeh! You are a bugger Maurice, always leaving me in the middle of the table!'

During a rehearsal in York Minster, Sir Michael Tippet was conducting his *Dances From Midsummer Marriage*. The harpist, not unknown to pluck out a rogue string, did so on this occasion! 'She's got her tits caught again!' said Maurice sitting next to me... which was followed by Sir Michael: 'Please do not do that my dear or you will unfortunately f**k the whole thing up!'

Playing in Britten's *Young Persons Guide to the Orchestra*, I turned to the drummer, Mike Blackley. 'As fast as you want for the trumpet variation,' I said to him, and he set the pace so fast that the conductor Maurice Handford threw his arms up, stopping in exasperation and exclaiming, 'How fast do you want this?' 'How fast can you move your arms?' Maurice Murphy quipped.

A scheme was set up by the BBC for promising young conductors to work with an orchestra, thus gaining valuable experience. The young Owain Arwel Hughes, whose father was head of music at BBC Wales, was at the back of the rehearsal room waiting his turn to conduct. Maurice Handford, affectionately known as 'Vinegar Joe' and then conducting the orchestra, was asked by the producer of the programme, 'Anything you want the apprentice to do, Maurice?'

'Yes! Ask him to go and clean my car. It's the third on the left down John Street'. Not until the head of music north, McDonald, retired some five years later did Handford conduct a BBC orchestra again.

George Hurst, known by the nickname of 'Black Jack', had a wonderful sense of creativity from a score, and his performances could be electrifying – although there could be a heavy atmosphere during his rehearsals.

The Milton Hall, where we rehearsed, was heated by a coke-stoked system. At times the hall would become unbearable with the coke fumes. We had in our midst our own orchestral canary, Basil Barker. Basil was a second violinist who, suffering from the choking fumes, would faint and roll off his chair, indicating the time to evacuate the building!

George Cottam, a long-established member of the orchestra, still played the bass trombone with the handle, now considered to be a relic of the past. On a visit to the Lake District we were waiting to collect our room keys in our hotel in Kendal when George approached the young female receptionist and in his best Lancashire accent, said, 'Mr Cottam, BBC. Which room please? Have you included my poe?' The girls said 'Sorry – a poe?', 'Yes,' he replied, 'a chamber pot. Agnes and me always use a chamber pot!' The embarrassed young lady retired to check on George's request.

Another of George's idiosyncrasies was his fastidiousness, which was known to everyone. A new member of the orchestra had made his presence felt by his lack of personal hygiene and was not popular in the orchestra's changing rooms. George was overheard in conversation with Connie, a first violinist who always dressed impeccably, floating on a fragrance of expensive French perfume. She complained that there was a similar problem in the ladies changing room. 'There's no excuse for it, Connie,' said George, 'I wash my penis and testicles every day!' Rather shocked, Connie replied, 'I agree entirely George… but there is no need to be so explicit.'

The same young new member upset George very much (being a left-wing activist) when he refused to stand to attention when playing the National Anthem. George took particular exception, as his father had lost his life while fighting for his country at Gallipoli whilst serving in the Lancashire Fusiliers. George rebuked the young bassoon player, who was firm in his beliefs. It was another example of BBC politics when it was arranged for this young man to hold the contra bassoon, an instrument requiring the player to remain seated at all times, and thus the incident of the National Anthem was defused.

One year George approached me saying, 'You'll be playing "The Trumpet Shall Sound" for me at Saddleworth in this year's *Messiah*'.

'Oh yes – nice of you to ask me, George,' I politely replied.

'It's an afternoon performance then back to our house where Agnes will have tea waiting for us. After tea we will have time to go to my local. I am respected there, so wear a hat,' he said.

On the day, as promised, Agnes had the tea ready and was in the kitchen washing up the pots and I felt it only right to offer my help when in came George. 'What are you doing in there? OUT! Agnes is the only one that washes up in this house'. George had not only a broad Lancashire accent but an old-fashioned attitude to family life.

Bill Maney, the bass clarinet player of the BBC Northern Symphony Orchestra, had served with the band of the Cheshire Regiment during the Second World War. One morning in Italy, about to start rehearsing the *Poet and Peasant Overture*, several members of the band were detailed to draw their rifles and ammunition: they were then marched to a small yard, where they found a young solider of the Durham Light Infantry tied to an old chair. Evidently he had been found guilty of the murder of an Italian fruit and vegetable cart dealer, and sentenced to death. After their dreadful duty of the execution had been completed, they were marched back to join the band just in time for the final bars of the overture.

On one occasion, the orchestra flew to Douglas, Isle of Man, for a broadcast of *Friday Night is Music Night*. On our way from the airport in Douglas, we approached the famous fairy bridge, whereupon the bus driver politely suggested that it was customary to wish the fairies good day. This we did, apart from the voice of Len Foster, the principal clarinettist: 'what a load of bollocks.' As we collected our cases at the hotel, it appeared that one had been left at the airport, and a despondent clarinettist had to return to retrieve it. 'Don't forget to wish the fairies good day Len,' a voice was heard to say.

Before one summer break I was talking with two members of the bass section, Alistair Hume and Simon Carrington, discussing plans for the summer holidays. The lads told me they were going on a working holiday on a cruise ship as a singing group. The lads, all having studied at King's College Cambridge, had come up with a name for the group – The King's Singers. Eventually Al and Simon left instrumental music behind in favour of a very popular and successful future in group singing, but that's another story…

Apart from the odd 'gig' with The Halle and Liverpool Phil., the four years I spent with the Northern was mostly a 10.00 a.m. to 5.00 p.m. existence. Altogether an unexciting time – in the studio most of the time, and very little chance of any teaching. Time to move again. There was a welcome in the hillside…

eighteen

Wales, Wales

The position of principal trumpet with the BBC Welsh Symphony Orchestra in 1967 included extra perks; trumpet and cornet tutor at the Welsh College of Music and Drama, and later University College Cardiff.

In the bass section of the orchestra was another old friend, Guy Henderson, who had been a regular freelance player with the BBC Northern. Cardiff was a picturesque city and provided a modern spacious BBC TV Centre in Llandaff, quite the opposite from life in Manchester, and proffered a most pleasant, delightful, working atmosphere… things were looking up.

Irwin Hoffman, an American of Eastern European descent who resembled a movie gangster, would usually conduct with his wife, Esther Glazier, the violin soloist. Irwin had a pair of enormous feet and these would be seen overlapping the edge of the orchestral rostrum. He also possessed a pair of searching tartar–like eyes which would sparkle as he spoke. 'The last time I was here in Cardiff was in 1944 with an armoured division… hell on wheels… prior to going to the Normandy beachhead!' Immediately Tom Proctor, second trumpet, jumped to his feet gesticulating with both arms above his head. 'Daddy!' he cried.

The BBC planners had allocated a programme to each orchestra in the BBC and our contribution was Beethoven's 10th Symphony, known as *The Battle Symphony*. This was a rarely performed work, written by Beethoven in commemoration of Wellington's victory at Vittoria in the Peninsula. The setting for the performance was hired from a collector of memorabilia. This took the form of a small display of vegetation, greenery, guns and hundreds of period model lead soldiers which the cameras would pan in on, giving the effect of a real battle. Alternate shots would be of the different sections of the orchestra.

Unbeknownst to television management, a Centurion Tank dated circa 1960s was strategically placed within the ranks of the British Red Coats. A horn player taking part in the event took a quiet moment to place the offending article, intending to create more firepower.

Each prominent Welsh composer, giving their services free of charge, had been invited to compose a processional piece of music to commemorate the investiture of the Queen's eldest son, Charles, as the Prince of Wales, which was to take place at Caernarfon Castle in North Wales. There was one exception, William Mathias, who insisted that his professional status required payment. This was not forthcoming and subsequently he would forfeit his invitation to the palace.

After an early breakfast at 5.00 a.m. provided by Bangor University, the orchestra left for Caernarfon Castle, where the tightest security was in place. We had to be in our seats by 6.00 a.m. The VIPs began to arrive and I noticed Jiggs Jaeger, now a lieutenant-colonel, who was in charge of the Kneller Hall Trumpeters positioned on the battlements of the castle. Jaeger was in conversation with James Chichester Clarke, now elevated to the rank of Prime Minister of Northern Ireland. I had the opportunity of talking to Jaeger and was introduced once again to Chichester Clarke, but had to suppress the urge to enquire of him if he had heard from Count Basie lately.

Jaeger had chosen to totally ignore Brian Altham, who was then second trombone, but who had previously served in the Irish Guards under Jaeger. It was then I became aware of who the culprit was in the saga of the 'Black Boot Polish Affair'!

The investiture continued with the glitter of all the Welsh opera stars of the time, Gwynneth from the Royal College of Music days and Roland, this time without his euphonium. Together with contingents from the cream of the Welsh choral scene, the orchestra commenced an hour's concert at 11.00 a.m., which was given a worldwide broadcast over television and radio.

Very shortly after this magnificent royal event and during a lunchtime broadcast, Brian Altham told me that his wife had heard on the early morning news the announcement of the death of the celebrated military band conductor, Col. Jaeger. I felt it appropriate to write a letter of condolence to his wife Eileen and so telephoned the guard room at Kneller Hall for their address. The sergeant in charge was at a loss to understand the reason for my request stating, 'I have just saluted the colonel, who was at that moment conducting the band'. Exactly one week to the day I read the obituary of Col. Jaeger in *The Times* newspaper. Brian Altham's wife still insists to this day that she heard the announcement on the radio.

Occasionally the orchestra would give a concert from Aberystwyth University, where I would usually have tea with Sylvia and Peter Kingswood, my old friend from the Royal College of Music, and the CBSO days. Peter was now a teacher and member of the University String Quartet. My wife Suzie insisted that I take a large jar of lemon curd, which she had recently made. For convenience I put it in my case containing my evening dress. As I was not required until the second half of the concert, I arrived during the interval, with time to change. To my horror, the jar, which I had forgotten to deliver, had broken, covering the contents of my case with lemon curd, leaving me with only one option. On came the conductor, looking rather surprised and puzzled at my unconventional attire (brown corduroy trousers, and a blue sweater). However, he still proceeded to point in my direction indicating that I begin the opening bars of *Pictures at an Exhibition*.

There was a mutual agreement between the two principal trumpets of the BBC and the Welsh National Opera Orchestras regarding extra work. Consequently I was engaged to play the offstage trumpet calls in Beethoven's *Overture Leonora III* at one of the Welsh Opera Orchestral Concerts. This was to be conducted by the principal director of music, Richard Armstrong, later to be knighted Sir Richard.

After playing the 'calls' in several locations in the building, all of which had been suggested by him, there was still no pleasing him, as none of the positions were to his liking, being either too near or too far away. This was getting tiresome! I approached the conductor saying, I was prepared to try the calls in one final position. If this was not acceptable to him I intended to go home and spend the rest of the day in my garden enjoying the lovely weather!

Although all of this was highly amusing to the orchestra, who gave their usual shuffle of feet, their way of giving approval, it was obviously not acceptable to Richard Armstrong. He appeared to be highly embarrassed and later complained about me to the management. A decision was made that I should never be engaged again. Some time later I met Terry Lax, first trumpet with the orchestra and gruff fellow Yorkshire man. Terry told me he had managed to change their decision, but that there was one condition. 'What's that?' I asked.

'In future keep your f***ing mouth shut!'

nineteen

Gypsy Rose Lee's prediction comes true

I decided it was time to pay a visit to my home back in the North of England and to enjoy a pint or two in The Black Bull Inn at Haworth – reputedly frequented by Branwell Brontë some years earlier. It was a nice day in July and as I entered the busy pub I noticed a fair-haired young lady enjoying soup, totally oblivious of me standing at the bar with my pint. This was Susan Spencer, the local star of so many musicals and the sister of Marian with whom I had enjoyed dancing on lots of occasions in the 1950s. I had an uncontrollable desire to get to know Susan better, but she left the pub, having finished her lunch, leaving me with a short, but wonderful memory.

My marriage of thirteen years had ended, but I was still sharing a house in Wales with my ex-wife, who was shortly to remarry a singer from the Welsh Opera. I couldn't live there any longer, of course. So collecting my only possessions, which constituted of my collections of Haworth landscapes (a total of three), I said goodbye to my daughter Linda and son Timothy, casualties of an unpredictable and unforgiving profession with the need to succeed, regardless of the consequences. It was too late to mend bridges this time but I was determined it would never happen again.

The bass section were a heavy, formidable bunch of 'hombres' capable of undermining the confidence of the hardest conductor. Big John Bush, a basic Buckinghamshire lad, was reading his book when Owain Arwel was waiting to begin. 'Farmers' Weekly is it?' 'No!' said John, 'Steam engines!'

An arrogant German conductor rehearsing Mahler's First Symphony noticed a large double bass unattended, the bass player not being in his usual seat. 'Where is he?' the conductor asked. 'How can I conduct Mahler without a full bass section?'

'Back soon,' replied Big John, 'Taken Freddie and Bertie for a walk…' Freddie and Bertie were two small Lancashire Heeler dogs belonging to Guy Henderson who could often be seen enjoying a pint of beer in the Black Lion in Llandaff.

A regular occurrence for Guy, following a Friday lunchtime broadcast, would be to drive all the way up North to Haworth, where he was a founder member of the Worth Valley Railway Society. Steam trains were his delight. The memory of the fair-haired girl in the pub at Haworth never left me and by sheer chance we met again when I travelled up North with Guy on one of his steam-train jaunts.

'I am in the book,' she said, when I cheekily asked for her telephone number, so I looked her up. Susan Spencer, Sunhurst Close, Oakworth. I phoned her and arranged a date. The date was a foursome – keep it casual, I thought – with Susan, her sister Marian, myself and Guy Henderson making up the four. This evening would change the course of all our lives.

Guy Henderson with his wife
Marian, and my wife Suzie.

Marian and Guy were married in May 1975 and now live in retirement in Burnley, Lancashire. Susan, or Suzie, as she prefers to be known, agreed to be my bride and we were married at the Haworth church.

It was to mean a big move for Suzie to leave her home and friends to enter an alien, artistic environment in Wales. Before leaving the area we decided to buy a small cottage on Marsh Lane, Oxenhope, only a few miles away from Suzie's mother, Hilda, in Oakworth. Back in Llandaff with my new bride I resumed my BBC duties.

Kiri Te Kanawa was the next guest artist on Stuart Burrows' television series, always filmed during the weekends. Kiri was tired after having sung at Covent Garden the previous evening and typically, there was no one to meet her on her arrival in Cardiff. She made her own way to the studios and sat on stage engaged in a natural and humorous conversation with the brass section of the orchestra. The producer of the programme rebuked Kiri for having moved from the cross he had marked for film shots. As he turned to leave, she said 'excuse me, whoever you are. I am tired and hungry, but most of the time I am happy. What makes you so f★★★ing miserable?' Her remarks found their way around the BBC quite quickly, much to the amusement of all concerned – except the gentleman in question.

In the bar of the ill-fated *Herald of Free Enterprise*.

I was in the BBC Club Rooms one day when who should walk in but – yes, you've guessed it – Jim Pope. It transpired that Jim had also moved to live in Wales and was now working as one of the announcers on Harlech Television.

The principal percussionist, Dave Bibby, was under constant attack from the conductor, Eric Bergel, who emanated from the then Eastern Block, Germany still being divided. The entire BBC company were aware of the arrival of Mr Bergel, as rather than stay in a hotel, which was the norm, he took up residence in the 'green room' – the dressing room reserved for artists. He would hang his washing to dry outside the window, turning the appearance of the building into a flag ship.

Bergel, having undergone the obligatory study of percussion as a second instrument, was overpowering in his attitude towards Dave's playing. Also, previous to his conducting career, Mr Bergel had been a trumpet player and was beginning to include the trumpet section with his heavy-handed suggestions. A gentle word was required. I advised Dave when in view of the conductor to give an occasional movement of the wrist giving an impression of a karate chop, so he did! I said to Bergel, 'I am sure you will join all of us, Mr Bergel, in wishing Mr Bibby every success on his visit to Japan to collect his Seventh Dan Grade…' The conductor agreed that this was a most unique achievement and from that moment on would give a general wave of satisfaction upon mounting the rostrum.

In 1978 the orchestra crossed the Channel on the ill-fated *Herald of Free Enterprise* for three performances of Bach's *B Minor Mass in Bruges*. Free until the evening performance, I decided to catch the 5 a.m. train down to Ypres, on my departure passing the 'heavy brigade' retiring from the bar to their beds. Being a First World War buff, it was an ideal opportunity for me to visit a few places of interest. In a small cemetery just outside Loos, I found myself by sheer coincidence looking at the grave of John Kipling, Irish Guards; Rudyard Kipling spent his whole life trying to locate his son's grave, but unfortunately because of map references it was not found until twenty years ago. Having spent an enjoyable day, I returned to Bruges for Bach's great work.

Right: The headstone of John Kipling, Irish
Guards, killed in action aged eighteen at the battle
of Loos, 1915.

Below: Shaun Harrold and myself, BBC, 1978.

Her Majesty the Queen opening the New Welsh College of Music.

The college brass ensemble playing for the Queen.

Britten's *War Requiem* at Hofkirche, Dresden in 1980 with the BBC Welsh Symphony Orchestra.

Jimmy Galway, the flautist, had just left the Berlin Philharmonic Orchestra and was to undertake his international career as a soloist, when BBC Wales booked him for a concerto. During an interval of the evening's performance, Suzie, my new wife, was about to order our after concert drinks in the BBC Club when she was approached and politely invited to join Mr Galway for dinner.

When I saw Jimmy flirting with Suzie I marched up to him asking him what his intentions were! 'Oh no! Not you again!' he said, remembering me from our days in the Royal College of Music together. A great character, who went on to achieve his well-deserved stardom and knighthood.

Another notable, slightly eccentric character was John Rowley, head of BBC Wales. Always amenable and approachable, he showed a great interest in the workings of the orchestra, who were collectively known, rather ungraciously, as The Works Band! It was not uncommon to find him in the lift playing the spoons!

Then there was Woodbine Willie, alias Alwyn Jones, who became head of music for a short time and addressed everybody as 'pal' or 'boyo'. Eminent conductors and visiting high-ranking members of the music world would all be subjected to his renowned generosity of handing round his Woodbines.

Just before the Christmas break one year I was standing in the queue of the canteen, behind a person dressed as a gorilla, who I eventually recognized as my friend Derek Boot. Derek had his own TV show, singing along to his guitar, and was taking a break from the recording of his children's Christmas show. Half an hour later, while waiting in his dressing room to go on stage, he lit a cigarette which set fire to his gorilla suit (which had a back zip fastening). There was no one to help him get out of it and the fire caused him horrific burns. He was taken to Chepstow Burns Unit, but did not recover and sadly passed away.

The world of musical conductors is one of many colourful characters, and one of them was Norman Del Mar, the quintessential Englishman, affectionately known as The Mass of Life. Norman always demanded Full Power during rehearsals but was unable to enunciate clearly and would cry 'Just keep it Mezzo Farte!' while bouncing up and down on the rostrum. Preparing a live show from the Town Hall in Cardiff, Norman was changing his clothes and had stripped to his underpants. In walked a rather arrogant Welsh councillor insisting that Norman leave as they were about to have a council meeting. He unceremoniously threw Norman out of the room for all the gathering audience to see. Although the councillor was made to apologise for his rudeness, the damage had been done. It was a most embarrassing experience for Mr Del Mar.

In June 1978, Suzie became pregnant with our first baby, Giles, and the Queen officially opened the new Welsh College of Music at Roath Park!

The college brass ensemble, for which I was responsible, had taken part in several successful engagements and was gaining a good reputation. I was fully confident in the talented young brass players, brilliantly led on trumpet by my star student, Shaun Harrold, who was to become a successful professional and a life-long devoted friend.

I received a telephone call from the principal of the college, Mr Edwards, inviting the brass ensemble to take part in the concert prior to the opening of the college and for us to discuss the programme. 'What type of music have you been playing,' asked Mr Edwards. I replied that at the moment we were playing a lot of Scheidt. Edwards reeled in shock:

'No! No! We must think of something more appropriate than, did you say sh★te?'

'The Battle Suite by Samuel Scheidt, the early German composer,' I replied.

'Ah yes! How appropriate,' said Edwards, regaining his composure.

The day arrived for the opening of the college by Her Majesty. All the VIPs were assembled in an enormous room. A BOOM from a Chinese gong, together with a brass fanfare, announced the arrival of the Queen.

After the concert those taking part waited to be presented to Her Majesty Queen Elizabeth along with myself, proudly wearing my Brigade of Guards tie. I could not help but think 'has she recognised me from Horse Guards Parade or maybe Windsor?' As the Queen approached the brass ensemble Mr Edwards introduced me as 'an ex-member of your Guards, Ma'am'.

'Really! Which one?' asked the Queen.

'Irish Ma'am – with Maj. Jaeger!'

'Ah! Dear Jiggs!' replied the Queen, moving on to the next in line. The Duke of Edinburgh followed the Queen asking, 'Who the hell wrote that fanfare?'

'Dr David Harris, sitting over there,' I replied.

'I'll have a word with him,' said the Duke.

Giles Spencer Casson made his debut on 26 January 1979, at Airedale General Hospital, Keighley, West Yorkshire. (I preferred that my son would be able to play cricket for Yorkshire should he so desire). He came to live in Cardiff with his mum, Suzie, and dad, Colin. Due to the pressure of work I spent less time than I wished with my lovely new family. I decided the best thing was to move back North and that was final! To what, I had no idea, but I wrote three letters of resignation to the BBC, the Welsh College of Music and the University College Cardiff. It was a hell of a decision, but there it was… I had done it.

Before leaving the BBC I was asked by the East German television company to go to Dresden with the orchestra to take part in a performance of Britten's *War Requiem*. Dresden: a mixture of drab communist buildings, open spaces and blackened ruins was all that remained of Dresden's once beautiful Gothic architecture. The performance was to take place in the Hofkirche, soon to be rebuild to its original state. Another moving experience not dissimilar to that in Coventry.

twenty

Happiness at a price

So we said our farewells to Wales and settled in our little cottage on Marsh, Oxenhope.

Day after day I sat and mused. Had I made the right decision? What the hell was I going to do? I made contact with an old associate, Paul Greenwood, then a musical advisor with Leeds Education, who was most sympathetic and arranged for me to have a few teaching session in the schools. Only a temporary solution, but it was a bolt hole.

I came in from a long walk off the moors with young Giles when the telephone rang… BBC Symphony Orchestra London… was I available to play principal trumpet in Vaughan Williams' *Fourth Symphony* as a part of their 50th anniversary celebration televised concerts from the Festival Hall in London? One of my pet aversions is the *Fourth Symphony* as it has some evil exposed entries – and why me, up in Yorkshire?

I took the job, arriving at Maida Vale Studios for rehearsals. The politics and intrigues soon unfolded. Rozhdestvensky, the then principal conductor, had sacked John 'Jumbo' Wilbraham and paid off the two deputies that followed, being dissatisfied with their musical prowess. I rang Suzie to say that I could well be returning on the next available train north… but not before telling him what he could do with his Vaughan Williams! After running straight through the piece he lifted his arms in a satisfying gesture. 'Have a good rest… see you all tomorrow.' I had survived once again and continued to do so for the concert the following day at the Royal Festival Hall.

Maxwell William Casson was born on 1 August 1980 and joined the rest of the party on Marsh completing a happiness for many years.

After being imprisoned in a studio environment for so many years it was a relief to be able to work on my reputation as a freelance trumpet player. It was at this time that I was approached by Huddersfield University with an offer of a position as trumpet tutor where I stayed for the next twenty-five years. My normal days would be: working in the mornings with the BBC Philharmonic in Manchester, drive to Leeds for an evening performance with Opera North at the Grand Theatre.

Some of the happiest times of my career were spent in Scotland. Glasgow was the European Capital of Culture and a hive of musical activity. The many friends that I made, and the ever-present welcome I received, were unsurpassable.

The Scottish National Orchestra (now the Royal Scottish) were awaiting the arrival of John Gracie who was leaving the BBC Philharmonic, though not for three months. Eric Knussen, the orchestra manager, invited me to take over as temporary principal trumpet and I was delighted to accept.

The BBC Philharmonic Orchestra brass section, studio 7, Manchester.

The Scottish National Orchestra brass, recording Richard Strauss' *Alpine Symphony*.

Sir Alexander Gibson, the then resident conductor, contributed much to musical life, but was never popular with the orchestra. When the records we made were produced, he would always send me an autographed copy with grateful thanks; I always had the greatest admiration for him. At the end of my short time in office, I left with indelible memories of the friendliest of orchestras.

My chosen musical career was not without its dangers however… Arriving home early from Manchester one day I found a message from Ian Killick, orchestra manager for Opera North, asking me to go straight to a dress rehearsal as the offstage trumpet in *Pagliacci* had been dismissed and paid off for the forthcoming performances. The piece contained exposed and difficult intervals and playing in the darkness off stage he suffered the ultimate and I had a feeling of guilt at being the one called in to play in his place.

A week or so passed and I arrived at the new theatre in Hull for a performance of the opera which was on tour. I asked one of the backstage 'roadies' where the offstage trumpet and drum were to be situated. 'Just f★★k off quick,' he shouted at me, so I did, thinking I was still in the Guards and cursing this ignoramus. 'Sorry about that,' he said to me later. 'There was a ton weight descending right above where you were stood and I hadn't the time to be polite!'

Ten minutes late and none too popular I arrived at Hereford Cathedral for an offstage part in Verdi's *Requiem*. A certain Christopher Robinson, conducting, impatiently pointed to someone who was waiting to direct us into our positions. After a long climb into the dizzy heights of the cathedral we crossed a wooden bridge leading onto an extremely narrow ledge. Another trumpeter was already there, cowering and pressing his body against the wall some 10ft away from me. Being petrified, he could not move, let alone play a trumpet. All of 60ft from the ground we eventually managed to persuade him to move to safety and the decision for us to return to ground level and *terra firma* was thankfully received. Mr Robinson was surprised and

With Ian Coul, Paddy Addinal and Mark Mosley, BBC Philharmonic trumpet section.

disappointed at our return. 'All my trumpet players work up there,' he insisted, after we refused to return to the dangerous heights. After my suggestion that in future he should employ the SAS he agreed on 'ground level', where most performances take place.

On a lighter note, there was one occasion when three trumpet players were required to play fanfares as part of a televised concert from St George's Hall, Liverpool, with the pop group 'Echo and the Bunny Men'.

After the concert had finished we were asked to play more fanfares, but this time standing on a narrow ledge on the outside of the hall. The most courageous of the three, Roy Ramsbottom, being totally unafraid of heights, stood on the apex of the ledge with buses passing beneath resembling Dinky toys. This left Mark Mosely and myself, both refusing to set foot out on to the ledge, coming to an agreement to play standing near to our courageous colleague.

I was invited to join the Scottish Opera for a season, which included a production of Benjamin Britten's *Peter Grimes*. This has an extremely difficult third trumpet part, noted for its high register writing. It is usually played on the smaller D trumpet. After some consideration I agreed to take the offer, but thought there could be a problem as the conductor was to be Richard Armstrong, my old adversary from Beethoven's *Leonora*! What sort of reception could I expect?

On my arrival in Glasgow, Richard came straight across the room to me and shook me by the hand, offering me a most warm and friendly welcome! The past being buried, we went on to enjoy a wonderful season playing together with one of the friendliest and most respected orchestras I have known. The season finished with an enjoyable week in Portugal, playing concerts in Lisbon.

In 1985 I received an open invitation to join the BBC Philharmonic Orchestra in Manchester. Though I was enjoying my freedom, I realised that I was only nine years short of a full BBC pension. With a growing, hungry family to support, it seemed like a good idea and I accepted their generous offer.

Bill Greenlees, without the optics.

In the Foreign Legion with Ian Coul.

Alcoholic refreshments were always available at the usual party which was given before a flight to a foreign land. These were enjoyed by whoever wished to indulge. Bill Greenlees, the contra bassoon, and ex 9th Lancers, was the perfect host, providing a liberal quantity of refreshments at the start of a successful tour. When it became evident to the upper echelons of the BBC Management that spirit optics had been secretly installed by Bill Greenlees in his locker they gave instructions to have them removed. This however did not curtail pre-tour parties, which continued unabated.

During long tours in Europe – usually consisting of one-night concerts – three coaches would be provided for the orchestra. These were affectionately known as 'pond life', 'neurotics' and 'cancer wagon' ('Vargon'). Inhabitants of the latter – mostly brass and woodwind players with a few of the string section – had acquired a more courageous sense of adventure, albeit at their own risk. For the satisfaction of sleep or a quiet journey, pond life or neurotics was the advisable option. No sleep was allowed on the cancer wagon, usually full of blue smoke, and the bar opened indefinitely as soon as 'wagons roll' time had been declared.

Playing with the BBC Phil. in an old deconsecrated church in Perpignan, Southern France, I took the liberty of looking through the gates of a Foreign Legion Barracks during an interval. A tough Spanish looking sergeant addressed me, telling me that entry was NOT permitted under any circumstances: '4th Guards Regiment, London' was the password! There followed an invitation to the mess following the concert.

Apparently this was a recruiting depot for the 3rd Regiment and at that time my friend was the sole occupant, being the cook. He delighted in displaying his knife and the bullet wounds he sported, and when he shook hands with me an acute paralysis took hold. About to retire to Angola as a mercenary in a more peaceful role, he opened the bar. Six of us stood to attention and drank a toast to the 3rd Regiment Legionnaires, after which our little friend ate the glass!

New recruits.

Andy Schmidt with a new member.

A pre-concert drink, BBC Philharmonic in Modena.

We showed our appreciation by purchasing his regimental mugs and at 3.00 a.m. said goodbye – but not before we had sampled his hot Moroccan Special!

Shortly after our French visit, the celebrated French conductor Louis Fremeur, a quietly spoken and accomplished musician, came to England for a week's stay with the orchestra. He was thrilled with our story of Perpignan as during the Second World War his regiment was the 3rd Regiment Legionnaires.

During one of the regular tours with the BBC Philharmonic we arrived in Munich. Bill Greenlees, who had rather a morbid interest in the Führer, suggested a wet lunch in the Hoffbrau House – the infamous beer cellar where Hitler began his early days of oratory. We sat on long wooden tables and joined the Bavarians clashing their Steiner glasses and swaying to the music of Andi Schmid und die Blaskapelle Bayern Top. I approached Andi and asked if I could have a blow with his band. He was delighted, passing me a trumpet and asking what I would like to play. 'Old Comrades,' I suggested, and off we went in oompah mode.

During the performance it was apparent that a great deal of laughter was coming from one of the gangways; Bill Greenlees was performing the Goose Step with arm outstretched in the Nazi salute. However, it did not amuse all present.

Playing at the Three Choirs Festival in Worcester, I stayed in Malvern with my old Army buddy, Pat Purcell of the Sydney Arts Ball fame. Pat had retired as a sergeant in the Micks and was now assistant music master at Malvern College. He promised to show me around the school and introduce me to some of the students the following day, which would be followed by elevenses in the headmaster's study.

BBC Philharmonic relaxing in Rio.

The BBC Philharmonic brass early morning rehearsal, Patras Fes Festival.

Also visiting and present at the elevenses was the headmaster of Eton. 'How is your life Charles? Are you truly contented?' asked the Eton Head. His friend, the head of Malvern, replied, 'Happy, apart from two things I have never experienced! Buggery and Morris Dancing! The two of course are not dissimilar!'

After a concert in Cologne, Germany to celebrate Henze's sixtieth birthday, the trumpet section retired to the hotel bar. Having had our fill by 3.00 a.m., we all took the lift to our bedrooms. We were surprised to find one bedroom door wide open. 'They are probably still celebrating,' said one of the lads, and we all walked into the room to find a naked female viola player draped over a chair. From the large bed in the room there appeared no movement until the sheets were pulled back…

'Well, what have we got here?' A member of percussion, an eminent political orchestral member and their naked female colleagues from the violin section!

'Any one got any booze?' asked one of the trumpeters.

During a break between rehearsal and concert performance at the Promenade Concerts held in the Royal Albert Hall, London, I went to the Television Centre to meet up with a friend who was taking part as a stand-in at a rehearsal of the show *Blankety Blank,* hosted at that time by Les Dawson.

I bumped into the rotund figure of Mr Dawson as he was enjoying a drink in the bar of the TV Centre. In conversation he told me about his many experiences while performing in the various towns and cities in the north of England. He had a special fond memory of working in the Keighley Hippodrome, a theatre in the town near to my home, long since demolished in favour of a bus station! I spent an unforgettable hour with the most modest and yet funniest man I have ever had the privilege to meet.

I have mentioned the political intrigues which seemed to be a normal part of professional musical life. I was nevertheless shocked to learn of the accepted practice of internal love affairs which were carried out during long tours of foreign countries, the people involved returning innocently to their respective spouses. The viola section was a magnet for ladies who preferred a more colourful personal life, although an understanding male would occasionally be accepted.

It was not uncommon for some players to take an extra case when on tour, which would be full of sandwiches. They would also attend a full self-service early breakfast at 6.00 a.m. and return at 9.45 a.m. for a refill! A certain bass player could often be seen collecting the plastic cups left scattered around after the tea break. He would wash them in the toilet and take them home for his children's birthday parties.

There was a group of individuals within the orchestra who became known as The God's Squad, being born again Christians. When on tour with the orchestra they would hold their morning bible meetings leaving the door of the room ajar, should any other member of the orchestra feel the need for more spiritual guidance. It was my habit to buy a daily national paper to read on my journey to Manchester. Quite often, not having had sufficient time to read it all while travelling, I would leave the paper in my trumpet case while rehearsing. I became increasingly annoyed when a member of The God's Squad saw fit to remove the paper, without asking my permission. One day after a tea break, I returned to my seat, to find him reading my paper; he had taken it yet once again. Being extremely annoyed, I sarcastically asked him if was he interested in a business proposition and offered to sell him the paper at half price, after I had finished with it. To my astonishment he accepted my offer, so I went to my locker, where I had amassed a large number of old copies of daily newspapers. I removed the front and back sheets and inserted an old edition of the paper, probably two or three months out of date. I then sold it for half price to the offender. I continued to do this every day to the end of my time at the BBC Philharmonic. I do hope that the financial situation of the offender has improved and that he is now able to afford an up-to-date copy of the daily paper.

Having a lunch break in the BBC Club one day just before Christmas, the topic was what the films would be shown on TV over the festive season. Someone said it would be the usual rubbish like *Zulu* and *Bridge on the River Kwai.* 'Hold on!' I said, 'Just a minute! I was in that film.'

Everyone present laughed with disbelief.

Someone must have taken me seriously, as some days later I received a telephone call from a television researcher working for a producer on an early evening programme called *FAX,* hosted by Bill Oddie. The programme was intended to answer questions that the general public might like to submit. I was told that at a Burma Star reunion the question had been asked whether the whistling of Colonel Bogie March had been performed by service men or actors. As I had claimed to be involved, could give any information? I put the young lady in touch with the band office, Irish Guards, Chelsea Barracks.

A few weeks later Suzie and I received an unexpected invitation to a television recording of the show. It seemed like a pleasant day's outing for us, so we travelled to the studios in Manchester in time for the afternoon runthrough when Bill Oddie briefly explained to us what form the programme would take. I was warned that, as a member of the audience, it was possible I could be asked about *The Bridge on the River Kwai* whistling incident.

Returning to our seats for the evening show I was surprised to be invited on to the stage. I went, albeit very reluctantly. Bill then asked me a lot of questions about how it had come about that I had been involved in the *Whistling March* as part of the musical track to the film. I explained to him, as I have already mentioned in this book, that it was a job that had to be done, and we the members of the Irish Guards Band at that time had done it, being paid the princely sum of £6!

Bill Oddie then asked how long it had been since I had been in touch with my fellow whistling colleagues. I answered that it must have been as long as thirty years. Then, as the cameras zoomed into a shot of Buckingham Palace with the present band playing *Colonel Bogie,* on marched my old buddies who, unknown to me, had been found, contacted and assembled especially for the programme. What a wonderful surprise, and another evening I shall never forget.

The stone plaque
presented to me by
Wilf Bottomley.

Above: The conclusion of the book party, Grand Canaria.

Left: Myself and Suzie at home in Marsh.

Sadly, politics rose to the surface yet again, when on the following day I was approached by the chairman of the Philharmonic Orchestra Committee who expressed his disappointment in me failing to mention the fact that I was a member of the BBC Phil. and giving them a bit of free publicity. After fulfilling my contract with the BBC Philharmonic I took retirement. No golden handshake or souvenir watch for me, after twenty-five years of service. Only a short, but nevertheless appreciative, letter from the head of music saw my departure from the organisation.

Semi-retired and still teaching, it was back to freelancing, with many enjoyable engagements travelling abroad with the London Symphony Orchestra, together with my old friends Maurice Murphy and Bill Lang. Bill, getting on a bit, was about to retire. Travelling back from Brussels after concerts in Europe, my companion was John Fletcher, probably the finest tuba player it has been my privilege to hear, and one of the most modest of Yorkshiremen. Tragically John died the day after returning home from that trip.

One of my last engagements was with the Manchester Camarata. I had been booked to play with them for a concert in Harrogate when I received an urgent call from the 'fixer' in a panic. Did I know a trumpeter? Someone had reported sick! I did know of someone – Bill Lang! Bill, who was in his eightieth year, had been retired for some time and was living in Harrogate. I telephone him on behalf of the fixer to ask if he was interested in the job. Of course he was, but naturally he had a few doubts, not having played in public for seven years. I was able to convince Bill that everything would be fine and we played together for what would be the last time.

I was still teaching at the Huddersfield University. I took it upon myself to ask the principal of the music department what my future position was and what the age limit for teaching at the university was. 'Sixty,' he replied, 'but you are pushing it at sixty five. Why do you ask?'

'Because I am seventy,' I said.

'Good Lord!' he exclaimed, 'You have been here ten years too long!'

'But you have paid me,' I said, 'Farewell!' And so my playing career came around full circle. I could still hear my father's voice, as I left home embarking on my adventures so many years before... 'If owt goes wrong tha can allus cum 'ome lad to your work.'

An old man of eighty-eight years, who I had known since childhood, approached me with a request. His name was Wilf Bottomley, a local stonemason, and his request was for Handel's *Largo* to be played at his expected funeral. Money was not an issue and I explained that I did not want a fee!

Shortly afterwards a brown, hand-painted, 'B' registered Reliant Robin accompanied by a few whiffs of brown smoke and a 'bang' came to a halt outside my door. 'I want you to accept this,' said Wilf. 'It's the last thing I will ever make.' It was a beautiful white stone plaque. A carving of a trumpet and the words 'Trumpeter what are you sounding now?' Within a week I had fulfilled his request.

I was increasingly aware that the 'the pond was beginning to dry'. With many talented youngsters in an already overcrowded market and my own teething problems I decided it was time to call it a day and hang up the trumpet.

Now I am able to enjoy my family and my time in the beautiful surroundings of my home in the Brontë countryside. One day, whilst on a walk, I stopped for a pint of the local brew, at the 'Wuthering Heights', a pub in Stanbury. Who should I see sitting at the bar with a pint in front of him but JIM POPE, also retired and also returned to Haworth. What a small world!

Sadly this was the last time that our paths crossed as Jim passed away shortly after this last meeting. Thus started a very poignant time in my life, with so many dear, beloved friends, associates and family passing away. Whilst enjoying some winter sunshine with my lovely Suzie holidaying in the Canary Islands with friends, I learnt of the death of my old friend and mentor, Bill Lang. Stonemason, tank driver, cornet player and trumpeter... He was the best!

Another close colleague, Barry Latcham, who had played second trumpet with the Bournemouth Symphony Orchestra for thirty years, also passed away. Barry and I had first met in the canteen at the Guards depot in Caterham and we marched many a mile through the streets of London together.

I can remember, as a very small boy, seeing a beautiful lady in our village. Little did I know that someday she would be the most wonderful, considerate and kindest mother-in-law to me and grandmother to my two boys, Giles and Max.

Referred to as 'the cavalry', Hilda was always there in times of need and had been widowed when her husband Walter, a well respected builder and singer, died at an early age. The only boy in the family was Paul, who welcomed me into the family without any question and has always been a tower of strength. Sadly, Hilda is no longer with us but along with my own parents left behind memories of love and affection.

The boys have flown the nest and Suzie continues exasperatedly but lovingly tolerating this mad musician. We still live in our little cottage on Marsh.

Colin Casson